WOODLAWN'S MODEL CITIES PLAN

WOODLAWN'S MODEL CITIES PLAN

A Demonstration of Citizen Responsibility

By: The Woodlawn Organization

Remarks By:

REV. ARTHUR BRAZIER
President, The Woodlawn Organization

MORRIS JANOWITZ
Professor, Department of Sociology
University of Chicago

JULIAN H. LEVI
Professor of Urban Studies
University of Chicago

LEON D. FINNEY
Staff Director, The Woodlawn Organization

JACK MELTZER
Director, Center for Urban Studies,
University of Chicago

*Publishers/*WHITEHALL COMPANY
601 Skokie Blvd./Northbrook, Ill.

Copyright, © 1970 By

WHITEHALL COMPANY
601 Skokie Blvd./Northbrook, Ill.

All rights reserved. No part of this book may be reproduced in any form, by mimeograph, xerox, or other means, without permission in writing from the publishers.

Library of Congress Catalog Card No. 74-84002

Manufactured in the United States of America
SBN 87655-010-3

"T.W.O." is pledged to take the initiative in the development of adequate standards and values for community living and to see that they are maintained. We recognize that the dynamics of an urban society calls for attentiveness and action if the well-being of the community is to prevail. To this end is "T.W.O." committed and pledged, and shall unrelentingly pursue this course.

Constitution as adopted March 24, 1961

TABLE OF CONTENTS

Remarks by Rev. Arthur Brazier, *President, The Woodlawn Organization*	3
Remarks by Morris Janowitz *Professor, Department of Sociology,* *University of Chicago*	10
Remarks by Julian H. Levi, *Professor of Urban Studies,* *University of Chicago*	15
Remarks by Leon D. Finney, *Staff Director, The Woodlawn Organization* *and* *Jack Meltzer,* *Director, Center for Urban Studies,* *University of Chicago*	20
INTRODUCTION	23
Model Cities Planning	23
The Key to Inner-City Problem Solution	25
The Woodlawn Setting	27
The Woodlawn Organization	29
Model Cities Plan— Organization and Process	32
Summary	35
Part I: PROBLEM STATEMENT	37
Woodlawn's Problem: Root and Proximate Causes of Poverty	37
Service, Health and Education Deficiencies	42
General Service Deficiencies, including Financial Assistance	42

CONTENTS

Health Deficiencies	47
Employment Deficiencies	50
Existing Manpower Program Deficiencies	50
Additional Economic Deficiencies	52
Other Deficiencies	55
Multiple Administrative Districts	55

Part II: GOALS, OBJECTIVES AND STRATEGIES:FRAMEWORK OF THE MODEL CITIES PLAN — 57

How the Plan is Constituted	57
Operational Measures	60
Goals and Objectives	61
Strategy	63
Overall Strategic Considerations	63
Strategic Framework	66
The Core and Outreach System:	
The Core	66
Outreach (The Pads)	79
The Education System	85
Housing and Economic Development	
Corporation (HED)	86

Part III:PROGRAMMATIC COMPONENTS — 91

The Core Divisions	92
Health Division of the Core	93
Ambulatory Health Services	100
Outreach Facilities (PADS)	101
Community Health Center	102
Inpatient Services	106
Acute Hospital Facility	106
Extended Care Facilities	108
Training Within the Health Facilities	110

CONTENTS

Immediate and Long Range Aims	110
Social Services Division of the Core	111
Organizational Framework for Social Services	113
Access Services	114
Self-support Services	115
Services to Mothers and Their Children	115
Services to Strengthen Family Life	116
Cultural Services	116
Protective Services for Children	116
Adult Protective Services	117
Rehabilitation Services for Blind and Disabled Adults	117
Financial Services Division of the Core	118
Who is Eligible	118
Reception and Application	119
Eligibility Determination	119
The Financial Grant	120
The Emergency Service Unit	122
Referrals to the Social Service Network	123
Clerical and Accounting	123
Law Division of the Core	126
Outline of the Woodlawn Services Program	126
The Individual Components	126
The Structure of the Woodlawn Legal Services Program	127
The Individaul Components in Detail	127
The Legal Aid Bureau	127
The Independent Neighborhood Law Firm	129

CONTENTS

The Neighborhood Education and Conciliation Council (NECC)	130
Community Organizations	132
The University of Chicago: Mandel Clinic	132
Environmental Planning Division of the Core	133
Education	138
Preschool Centers	143
Primary Schools	144
Middle Schools	146
Hyde Park High School	147
The Fluid Schools	148
Cultural and Language Arts Center	150
Recreation Center	151
Housing and Economic Development and Employment	151
Priorities	154
Feasibility of Achieving Results	155
Career Preparation Within the HED	157
The Three Settings of Career Preparation	160
Special Programs	167
Related Proposals	170
Housing and Economic Development Functions of the HED	172
Industrial Park	172
Small Business Service Program	174
Housing	180
Program for Young People	184
Part IV: FIRST YEAR ACTION PROGRAM AND CONCLUSION	187
The Major Areas of First-Year Activities (Seven Elements)	187
Action Components in the First-Year Program	189

CONTENTS

APPENDIX—T.W.O.   192

APPENDIX—U OF C   199

APPENDIX—TASK FORCE   204

WOODLAWN'S MODEL CITIES PLAN

WHAT KIND OF MODEL CITIES?
By
Rev. Arthur Brazier, President
The Woodlawn Organization

I shall address my remarks to what I consider the major prerequisites for a successful Model Cities program in Woodlawn. But first, let me make it clear that when I refer to a "successful" program, I mean successful from the point of view of the people of Woodlawn, the people who are to participate in and to be served by this program. Black Americans have learned through many years of bitter disillusionment that they no longer can permit others—however friendly they may be—to define our needs, nor can we permit others to solely determine how these needs should be administered or satisfied. While we welcome the help of our friends, we cannot abdicate our responsibility to ourselves.

Therefore, I shall not speak to the technical requirements of this program. I shall confine my remarks to questions of the relationships of powerful components, their basic postures, their underlying attitudes, their primary motivations, and, if you will permit me to sound a bit paranoid, I shall allude to ulterior motives that could destroy the program in its infancy.

The Model Cities concept in general terms—is a beautiful and timely projection. A bit late, but still a great idea. What black man could be against its multi-faceted community services? What black man could reject the idea of a concentrated attack on poverty, inferior education, unemployment and slum housing? Who among us could oppose more legal aid for the defenseless, better health services for the poor—just to mention a few ingredients of the Model Cities idea. I say again, no one is against such a program in principle.

*Speech delivered to Conference on Delivery Systems, Spring, 1969, convened by Center for Policy Studies and Center for Urban Studies.

However, we are concerned with the application of these programs; how and by whom these programs are going to be administered; the extent and depth of the financial commitment to these programs; and who will have the determining, ultimate voice in the structuring, and crucial decision-making processes involved.

Why has The Woodlawn Organization raised the controversial issue of community control rather than just moving ahead and getting some of that government money and expertise into Woodlawn? In the first place, money alone will not answer our needs, and secondly, some experts loose their expertise when the question of race appears on the drawing board. All plausible arguments to the contrary notwithstanding, now is the time to settle all the questions that I have raised.

The present Model Cities concept is not the first noble idea presented supposedly to help the disadvantaged. The history of modern urban society is replete with the failures of ideas of equal worth and urgency advanced by some of the most prominent names in their respective fields. Most of them had one thing in common; they thought that they, and only they, were capable of working out the solutions to our needs.

A "delivery system" to them meant for black people to sit quietly by while they, with alternatingly warm and stern paternalism, delivered to us what they thought we needed. To them, our advice and consent was not needed, and when volunteered, it was not heeded.

At this moment my mind goes back to the 1930's when the concept of public housing became a reality. The only people who opposed public housing AT THAT TIME were the conservatives who were either frightened by the spectre of socialism or who just didn't want to see the government spending money on poor people—black or white. Many people remember the completion of the Ida B. Wells Homes. It provided a sort of model public housing program for that decade. It received much public approval throughout the land. And it was a truly great, humane idea. It took thousands of overcrowded blacks out of intolerable conditions and provided them with neat, new apartments with rents to match their incomes. Witness, however, what actually happened. Public housing was converted into a compound for poor, powerless, and politically exploited black people. But to large numbers of white Chicagoans, public housing is a success. It keeps large numbers of overcrowded blacks from spilling over into lily white neighborhoods. But to the people who must live in these compounds, public housing is a failure when it crams 27,000 poor people within the confines of a compound like a Robert Taylor Homes.

Public housing is a dismal failure if you are a mother trying to rear small children from a highrise apartment. Public housing is a failure when its stultifying social climate turns blacks against blacks in daily outbursts of violence. It is significant that some of the most violent of racial explosions of the past four years occurred in or around some of these public housing compounds.

When we look back at public housing we must raise the questions of goal orientation and the ulterior motives that I spoke of earlier. And from the vantage point of the present, it is candidly clear that the powers who finally determined the character and course of public housing in this city gave little thought to the plight of the people who would occupy those buildings. They were preoccupied with other overriding considerations, to wit: the maintenance of segregated housing in Chicago. Of course, the city fathers had other very practical goals in mind, too; however, none of their goals gave priority to the crying needs of the people who live out their lives and bring up their children in a public housing project.

The same can be said of slum clearance and urban renewal. Everybody is against slums, and who could oppose the renewal of our cities? We were introduced to the concept of urban renewal in the late 1940's. It was hailed by some of our best minds as a savior of the cities. In 1948 we got a chance to see urban renewal in action in the communities adjacent to Michael Reese Hospital. Even then, many blacks suspected that this was not urban renewal but "Negro Removal". But they were drowned out and overridden by the establishment. Some of our white friends accused the black protester of being too sensitive, biased and shortsighted.

In 1969, it is reasonable to say that the people who determined the character of urban renewal in the Michael Reese Hospital-Illinois Institute of Technology area were not concerned with the plight of the black people who lived there before renewal. They were primarily concerned with maintaining the hospital and school as viable institutions and making the surrounding communities compatible with the growth plans of those institutions. They were concerned with reclaiming valuable land in close proximity to the loop and the lake. They were concerned with the low tax yield of the property in the community, and they were alarmed about another white problem common to nearly all big cities—the flight of white residents to the suburbs. In the midst of all these concerns, the powerless black population was not merely pushed to the back of the bus; it was pushed off and left to its own devices. In 1948, to have suggested that this would happen would have meant that one was paranoid.

The so-called success of South Commons Development has been heralded in the headlines of the Chicago Daily Defender issue of April, 1969, which reads, "South Commons Luring Many Families Back from the Suburbs," and is echoed in the statements of that community's management group. The fact is that the overwhelming number of new residents being lured back to this old black community will be white with a sprinkling of blacks just for the record. Yes, urban renewal at South Commons is a *success* for those whose primary motivation is to make the world nice and comfortable for the middle class. But what about the blacks who once lived there, the blacks who had no voice in the development of their community?

The same can be said of another wonderful idea— the F.H.A. home loan. Initially, blacks thought that this would be a boom to black ownership, since F.H.A. was designed to help people purchase homes with small down payments, reasonable rates of interest and long-term amortization. Thanks to F.H.A. we would be able to purchase adequate housing throughout the city, anywhere, because we no longer would be at the complete mercy of loan sharks and prejudiced mortgage institutions. That didn't happen. Our federal government, through F.H.A., simply made it easier for whites to flee the city to the suburbs—extending segregation to the countrysides—and now through urban renewal and black removal it is making it easier for these same people to return to the city and live in communities taken from blacks.

Suspicion was and still is a part of the climate whenever we hear of any program involving government funds or powerful white institutions. When the highly laudable War on Poverty program was announced, once again we were suspicious. Did white America really intend to do something about hunger or was its main purpose the offering of a few tranquilizers to restless, riot-prone black communities? Shocking front page stories in our nation's dailies about the thousands of black children still suffering brain damage because of a lack of protein justifies our suspicions. And, if additional confirmation is needed—there is the report of the survey on Operation Head Start which shows that most children in the program are hardly better off than before.

Right here I must ask, did that noble idea of a national War on Poverty become more concerned with protecting the political status quo than with the hunger of the poor? I recognize that many poor people have been helped by all of these programs, but I suspect that they represent only a fraction of the needy. The Model Cities program can become just another failure in a long chain of failures because the program is clouded with suspicion and the burden of removing that suspicion must be placed on the shoulders of the governmental agencies involved and the major private institutions. The governmental agencies must convincingly show that they are concerned with the community's people rather than with politics. And by the same token, the powerful institutions must convincingly demonstrate that they too are primarily concerned with the people who are their neighbors as well as the long range goals of the institutions. That overall climate of trust does not exist today.

We need a fresh start—a beginning based on tangible, permanent, and sincere examples of respect and concern for the people of Woodlawn, Lawndale, Uptown, Kenwood-Oakland, Grand Boulevard and any other community where Model Cities programs are contemplated.

The Woodlawn community deserves and is in dire need of ample government funds. At the same time, the University of Chicago has unduplicated technical know-how that should be made available to the Woodlawn community. On the other hand, both the government and the University cannot fulfill the hopes embraced in the Model Cities concept without the first-hand knowledge and experience of a self-determining Woodlawn community.

I am exceedingly happy to report that the Woodlawn community and the University of Chicago have taken the first step in the direction of mutual understanding and cooperation. Over the past few years, T.W.O. and the University specialists in law, urban planning, social welfare, medicine, economic development, and education have been working together in the development of a meaningful Model Cities program with the University working under the direction of the Woodlawn community. This is how it should be; in fact, this is the only way it can be.

Lest anyone misunderstand, it should be clearly pointed out that within the Woodlawn community there remains a certain amount of hostility and suspicion toward the University. The long years of conflict and confrontation between the University of Chicago and the Woodlawn community have not been forgotten by many of its residents. There are many who believe that the University's ultimate goal is clearance of Woodlawn and a rebuilding designed for middle class white and black residents. It is incumbent upon the University to dispel this lingering suspicion and hostility.

What we have here in the T.W.O. plan is a Model Cities program in which the organized community has played a meaningful and determining role. It is a program designed by the people of Woodlawn for the people of Woodlawn.

REMARKS
By
Morris Janowitz, Professor
Department of Sociology
University of Chicago

The volume presents a plan for improving the life conditions of the citizens of Woodlawn by means of increasing their self-determination and community control. The citizens of Woodlawn are not seeking to create a self contained island. They are using the concepts of community control in order to enter into the main stream of American society.

This report is the work and expression of the citizens of Woodlawn. It represents their effort to define their social and economic problems as they experience them. In the ongoing process of preparing this document, individual members of the faculty and student body of the University of Chicago were asked to contribute their technical expertise.

The faculty of the University of Chicago believe that its primary tasks are intellectual. Their work centers on research, scholarship and classroom teaching in order to transmit and enrich our cultural and scientific tradition.

At the same time, many of the faculty as individual citizens believe that they have other roles to perform and that with care, these tasks can be carried out without weakening their academic responsibilities. The efforts of faculty members and students of the University of Chicago to assist in the preparation of this Model Cities Plan by The Woodlawn Organization is one such task.

It is fashionable in university circles to speak of the

need for public service in the larger society, but in the many months of work on the Model Cities planning document, this phrase was never consciously used by any party. In the language of The Woodlawn Organization, the faculty and students of the University of Chicago served as "technicians and consultants" to a community organization.

This means that faculty and students recognize their obligation to insure that their skills will be utilized in the broadest public interest and not be restricted to any particular privileged or special interests. Because the University of Chicago exists in the midst of a vast metropolitan concentration, the faculty and students are citizens of a local community and have special responsibilities as neighbors to the adjoining communities.

In a period of rapid social change, the classroom and scholarly journals do not suffice as channels of communication. Some members of the faculty must make their professional expertise and knowledge directly available to community groups in the inner city. The University of Chicago has a long tradition of research in the urban setting, and an unbroken line of faculty members who have worked with community organizations. However, these experiences are hardly an effective guide to involvement in the contemporary issues of the black community. During this Model Cities program, the faculty and students of the University of Chicago were learning as much as serving.

Through the summer and fall of 1968, work on the planning document proceeded with great intensity. At all times, it was clearly emphasized that, although each faculty and student was a member of the University of Chicago community, they served as individuals. They were not on assignment from the University administration. As individuals they were aware of the complex and stormy history of university and community relations in Woodlawn. They did not serve as outside experts removed from the problems and issues of Woodlawn who were engaged in a single shot "professional visit." Each faculty member had some previous involvement in Woodlawn developments, and some had worked for many years. These personal and professional commitments are certain to continue regardless of the outcome and impact of this particular Model Cities plan.

What did the faculty and students actually do as "technicians and consultants?" First, they served as resources of factual data which would have been difficult for the community to assemble. They were able to mobilize basic information about the community from official and unofficial sources and from specialized studies. They had at their disposal knowledge about the structure of private and public agencies outside the community and especially important, information about previous and ongoing programs of community development in other local areas. Second, they offered conceptual knowledge about the social process and about alternative structures and strategies of planned change. Third, the Model Cities program requires specific research tasks to be designed to assist in implementation and evaluation of the program. The consultants offered technical assistance in meeting these aspects of the planning document.

The Center for Urban Studies, under the direction of Jack Meltzer, was the device for assembling and managing these efforts. Faculty participation was therefore an uncompensated assignment, outside of university responsibilities. For most, this experience will no doubt influence their academic writing and classroom teaching.

The students who participated did so as research assistants and internes because of the obvious educational benefits to be derived.

Although faculty and students participated in the drafting of every section of analysis and documentation, every proposal is the end product of various committees of The Woodlawn Organization and its ruling bodies. We are pleased that The Woodlawn Organization has made special efforts to give this plan the widest possible distribution. The central concepts, for example, of citizen participation, consolidation of professional services, the use of indigenous personnel, and the fusion of educational and work experiences are and will be central efforts of community development in the decade ahead. We are also painfully aware that the real consequences of this effort depend on its acceptance, funding and implementation.

Some university administrators, faculty, and students believe that universities should be central planning agencies for social change in the big cities, in part because other agencies have failed. Both the University of Chicago community and The Woodlawn Organization reject this grandiose notion. The Woodlawn Organization does not believe that experts should determine policy. The faculty also rejects this notion because they are aware of the sheer inability of the university to undertake such ambitious tasks and because they are concerned with the need to maintain the autonomy and intellectual goals of the university. Therefore, the contents of this document are demonstrations of possible and realistic contributions of university faculty and students to a community organization engaged in meeting the urban "crisis."

REMARKS
By
Julian H. Levi, Professor of Urban Studies
University of Chicago

The Woodlawn Organization Model City Plan is a unique community document. The proposals made express community decisions determined not only by community committees but distilled through seven public hearings conducted by the community organization. In short, The Woodlawn Organization Model City Plan is the view of thousands of Woodlawn citizens.

The role of the University of Chicago Faculty-Student Task Forces was quite clear and limited. From the inception of the effort it was understood by all that while University Task Forces could counsel and advise, the community organization was the client. It must make the policy decisions. Accordingly, the community determined not only what remedial action should be advocated, but even the particular community problems which must be regarded as crucial. The selection of the goals of improved education of the young, of improved employment opportunity, of income maintenance and social services, and of a decent home and a suitable living environment are community choices. The process was one of community decision and responsibility rather than passive, or even active, participation.

The raw social data supports these resolutions:

"Woodlawn is a community where one of every ten men cannot find a job; where six out of ten high school students drop out; where one out of three children born is illegitimate; and where one-quarter of its population is on welfare. Other statistics are equally depressing. Its infant mortality rates, venereal disease rates, and premarital birth rates are among the highest in the city. These conditions have been created and perpetuated by discrimination, neglect, and the endless denial of the population's potential."

Life experience of Woodlawn residents has taught them all too much about the indifference and the ineffectiveness of education, health, welfare, and employment systems which, however well conceived, are administered at the convenience of the supplier rather than as service to the consumer.

The Model City proposals, moreover, are the sum of much more than the comparatively short months of specific Model City planning effort. For more than five years the Department of Psychiatry of the Pritzker Medical School of the University of Chicago has operated the Woodlawn Mental Health Program in cooperation with the Chicago Board of Health, but under the auspices and direction of a policy board of community residents. That policy board decided that the program should be undertaken, that it should concentrate on children, and that it should seek entry at the first grade of all elementary schools in Woodlawn. That board approved the selection of the schools for treatment and the schools for control. It approved organizational arrangements, the employment of community agents, and even the location of the office. Accordingly, for each of the past five years between 1,400 and 2,000 children in first grade have been seen.

Similarly, the Department of Pediatrics of the Pritzker Medical School of the University of Chicago for approximately the past eighteen months has operated the Woodlawn Child Care Clinic, assisted by the Children's Bureau of the United States Department of Health, Education, and Welfare. Again, there has been the pattern of the community policy board, the employment of community agents, and the assumption of major decision responsibilities by community people.

In 1967 the Graduate School of Education of the University of Chicago, in collaboration with the Chicago Board of Education and The Woodlawn Organization, participated in the formation and operation of the Woodlawn Experimental School District, funded pursuant to Title III of the Elementary and Secondary Education Act and involving approximately 4,000 children at the Wadsworth Elementary and Upper Grade Center and at Hyde Park High School. The basic memorandum of agreement, approved by the three parties, provides that, subject to the general powers of the Board of Education and the General Superintendent of Schools as defined by state statute, the policy board will have essential powers and responsibilities over all phases of the operation of the Experimental District. Each party names seven representatives to the policy board, who caucus separately, with the requirement that determinations in the policy board be made with the concurrence of the majority of each constituent group.

Neither the University of Chicago faculty nor The Woodlawn Organization were strangers to one another. The proposals made are the product of day-to-day exposure over a number of years. The role of University faculty must, moreover, be understood as more than the voluntary, unpaid participation of interested citizens.

WOODLAWN'S MODEL CITIES PLAN

In their judgment the particular community problems are relevant to their own educational interests and responsibilities. Better systems of delivery of health or welfare care, or educational service, or justice are cogent to a medical school, a school of social service administration, a graduate school of education, or a law school. Processes of community growth and change, of deterioration and decline, of rejuvenation and rehabilitation are core issues to a center for urban studies.

The University of Chicago effort is distinct in collaboration achieved across many schools and disciplines. Jack Meltzer, Director of the Center for Urban Studies at the University of Chicago, together with staff, became the most effective focus in performance of the Woodlawn Plan. Moreover, faculty at the University long ago concluded that Woodlawn must not be regarded as a mere convenient laboratory and that research and educational efforts must be undertaken by them only under community sanction and aegis, in which the professionals were the junior partners. The experience has demonstrated, moreover, that research undertaken under these auspices is, in fact, far more productive than otherwise.

Contribution of the Student Task Forces was essential. These young people brought far more than deeply felt conviction and enthusiasm. Their own skills, sense of intellectual integrity, and hard work contributed flesh and sinew to otherwise sparse concepts. The partnership of University and community was supported by the partnership of faculty and students.

No participant in this effort is under illusion either as to the difficulties of approval or implementation of the proposals made, nor as to the rigors of the tasks involved. At this point in time, the Model City proposals represent only a private unofficial effort. Public approvals after full hearing are required of the municipal authorities, as well as of a variety of Federal departments and agencies. Further, while the funding proposed for the first year of operation would seem consistent with Federal allocations set aside for the city, future years are subject to the unknowns of Federal authorization and appropriation policies.

Finally, no one in the present state of knowledge can be confident about the detailed proposals. Woodlawn problems are not brick and mortar—they are people problems, not susceptible to immediate, or even rapid, solution. Three centuries of denial of civil rights, of inadequate and unfair allocation of public and private resources, of denial of human dignity and equal opportunity, cannot be reversed in five short years. The pragmatics are more simple. Progress, if made under community auspices and control, will be valued and prized; but if undertaken and directed exclusively by outside authority and agencies, will be rejected.

Despite a likelihood of failure, accepted by all, the effort was undertaken. Participation has been a privilege prized by all.

REMARKS
By
Leon D. Finney, Staff Director
The Woodlawn Organization
and
Jack Meltzer, Director
Center for Urban Studies
University of Chicago

The people who authored this plan have articulated new ways by which various professions and disciplines can relate to inner-city communities. The University participants, drawn from the professions and disciplines, who assisted the people in the plan's preparation, accepted as a basic principle the need to transform their respective fields in light of their recognition that conventional approaches were failing to meet the needs of residents in Woodlawn and in other inner-city areas.

In sum, the plan constitutes a program to adapt traditional fields so that the perception and goals of the inner-city resident comprise the central focus, rather than being bound by self serving professional definitions and purposes.

This T.W.O. Model Cities Plan sets forth an approach which leaves citizens, the consumers of services, the prime responsibility for making critical decisions which affect their lives. Thus this plan stands in sharp contrast to conventional attempts which have sought to aid the inner-city resident by extending agency services and thereby perpetuating professional and political power centered in forces outside the community.

This plan, by retaining decision-making power within the community and by fostering and engendering self-determination and personal dignity, creates the climate for the professional to function and operate effectively. Thus the Plan seeks to change the "System" and the way in which the professional agencies operate within the system.

The changes sought are based on a set of principles which stress the central importance of the individual, family and community, as constituting the focus around which professional functions and governmental jurisdictions are ordered.

In this spirit, the current practice which demands that beneficiaries of services adjust their behavior to the dictates of the professions, is replaced by the requirement that the professions and agencies adapt their behavior to the dictates of the professions, is replaced by the requirement that the professions and agencies adapt their behavior to the needs of the community.

The Plan demands that each profession reexamine its own professional content and activity to separate those functions which constitute its special skills from those functions which are merely the result of historical accumulation and administrative inertia. In addition, each profession will find new horizons for commitment to functions which are not exclusively oriented toward service, but are rather directed toward training and changing institutional practice.

Consistent with these purposes, the T.W.O. plan seeks to apply and extend to all professional service areas the principle that every citizen be provided with the wherewithal to perform as a consumer and not as a client, which is the pattern in the larger society.

Increased community participation and control is frequently seen as a danger to the central city government.

WOODLAWN'S MODEL CITIES PLAN

It is thought that increased community participation will split and weaken unified city action by decentralizing and dissipating the power of the city government. The issue, however, as seen by the T.W.O. plan, is to achieve centralization at a variety of functional levels, including the central city itself whose powers are presently fragmented by independent agencies. These agencies have already imposed on the central city's communities decentralized patterns. What the T.W.O. plan seeks to achieve is a centralized layer at the community level in which functions are incorporated into, and controlled by the community. The result is the creation of new institutional relationships.

The current pattern assumes that service and operating measures are permanent and immutable, inevitably risking the frustration and despair which has too long characterized our public programs. While successes may not flow from all of the specific measures undertaken, the citizen is strengthened by knowing that it is his community he is restructuring—a community in which services and specific operating programs are flexible and replaceable.

This T.W.O. Model Cities Plan was not accepted by the City of Chicago or the Department of Housing and Urban Development. Rather, the city and federal government in the Spring of 1969 approved the plan prepared by Chicago's official city agencies. Nevertheless, this plan continues to constitute a basic framework for community development, not only for the Woodlawn community, but for other inner-city communities as well. It represents a reordering and restructuring of professional service in inner-city communities that may well set the pattern for real change in urban ghettos across the country.

INTRODUCTION

MODEL CITIES PLANNING

In May, 1968, the Woodlawn Organization took the first steps toward developing a Model Cities plan for the Woodlawn neighborhood. This is an account of the process of planning that emerged, and the plan that resulted.

The United States Department of Housing and Urban Development (HUD) had selected Chicago as one of the initial cities to receive Model Cities planning funds; Chicago in turn had requested and received approval to designate four Model Cities study areas throughout the city, instead of the customary one; and East Woodlawn was ultimately selected as one of the four target areas. Even though the East Woodlawn designation was based on artificial boundaries since the geographic segment marked off has clear and integral relationships to the west and southeast, we at T.W.O. looked forward optimistically (granted an historical basis for skepticism) to the promise associated with the federal Model Cities conception.

Unfortunately, the city government intended that our voice be used not in the service of Woodlawn residents, but to benefit other interests and other groups. For us to have accepted the conditions laid down for our involvement would have resulted in abandoning our goal of achieving responsible citizenship—the critical fulcrum required to solve the problems of Woodlawn or any inner-city community.

But a new excitement gripped us: Why not develop our own Model Cities plan? Although technical help was necessary, many University of Chicago faculty and students had long demonstrated a willingness to perform as technicians and consultants—and an equal willingness to leave policy and decision-making to the residents. If a first-rate plan could be drawn up, the city would have to take us seriously.

We said to the University: Woodlawn needs and wants a Model Cities plan that departs from the vague and variously interpreted term "citizen participation," and in its place stresses the principle of "citizen responsibility." We seek to prepare a plan which itself constitutes a dramatic demonstration of "citizen responsibility." It is not only a democratic planning process we seek, but a continuing and enlarging role for the residents of Woodlawn, the plan's consumers and beneficiaries throughout the undertaking. We ask that you, the University, not only aid in the process of planning, but be prepared to try to adapt yourself and the professional establishments with which you are associated to help make the plan successful.

We recognized that unlimited exercise of power by professional functionaries and practitioners had long been inadequate to meet the needs of Woodlawn. We saw that not only should citizens be held accountable to officials and professionals for their actions, but professionals and officials must be held accountable to the Woodlawn citizens they serve.

INTRODUCTION

Our central theme can be stated simply: *Ideas and money, private and public, become powerful weapons when put in the service of "responsible citizens"; but when applied independently, ideas and dollars are stopgaps at best and at worst the object of scorn and hostility.*

The University pointed out that it is a community of scholars—faculty and students. Such a community could not take on the role of technician and consultant or any other academically related function. While it welcomed and applauded T.W.O.'s desire to build on citizen responsibility, the decision to work with T.W.O. could be made only by individuals—not by the University as a unit. Faculty and students were then approached via the University's Center for Urban Studies; they responded with enthusiasm and excitement. It was clear that faculty and students, while confident of their special skills, were less certain that they could measure up to the demands of the community. Protectively, faculty and students made it very clear to us that "citizen responsibility" also meant "citizen accountability," and that technical advice and consultation, which would be provided as sought, left decisions among alternatives, refinements, elaborations, and final directions to the community. This admonition was to us a strength and constituted the basis we sought in our relationship.

In June of 1968 we launched our Model Cities planning with the technical assistance and consultation of University of Chicago faculty and students.

The Key to Inner-City Problem Solution

The essential ingredients in developing a workable

WOODLAWN'S MODEL CITIES PLAN

plan and program for an inner-city area are: (1) the assumption of responsibility by the affected community for the plan's preparation, and (2) the continuing central community responsibility, in coordination with the city government, during the period of the plan's undertaking.

Only when the residents of an inner-city area assume such responsibility during both the planning and the implementing stages can there be any hopeful expectation that available public programs (frequently launched with fervor) will achieve their promises and extend their benefits. Similarly, it is only under these circumstances that the expertise and skill of the professional can be expected to have the impact necessary to achieve discernible results. As a matter of fact, the failure to recognize the critical role of *citizen responsibility* exercised through accepted and recognized community organizations may account largely for the frustrating failures of public programs which deal with the problems of the inner city and the inability of professionals to use their knowledge in an effective way in the inner city. Government programs, public agencies and departments, and professionals cannot by themselves or in combination guarantee that social change will be effected in ways which are acceptable either to the inner-city resident or to society at large.

Allied with this pivotal reliance on citizen and community responsibility, this document attempts to achieve a more direct approach to the interplay between community needs and the professional by placing considerable emphasis on the organizational setting in which the professional will function. The "whole man" concept is used by The Woodlawn Organization. This concept dramatizes the need to treat community and personal

INTRODUCTION

problems as a whole and not in terms of conventional categories of education, medical care, social welfare, or legal approaches. T.W.O. sees as essential the necessity to fuse together the various skill specialists into working teams rather than continue the custom of "competing practitioners."

We seek also in this document to give conceptual and programmatic content to the central issues of decentralization. The basic thrust is that there is a real and fundamental difference between decentralization, a desired goal, and fragmentation, which would merely continue present weaknesses. In order to achieve effective decentralization, to make it possible for the individual citizen to reach central authority and vice versa, it is essential to develop centralized community-wide facilities. Consequently, decentralization of operations requires centralization and consolidation of many technical, professional, and support functions.

In short, this document is based on the belief that there is a convergence between the needs and statements of the citizens of Woodlawn and the concepts of the technical expert and social scientist. This document is an expression of the pragmatic outlook which has a long tradition in American life, but which has not been adequately related to the issues of the inner city.

The Woodlawn Setting

The preparation of this Model Cities plan by T.W.O. for the Woodlawn target area (East 60th Street on the north, East 67th Street on the south, South Cottage Grove Avenue on the west, and South Stony Island Avenue on the east, commonly referred to as the East

WOODLAWN'S MODEL CITIES PLAN

Woodlawn Area) is the logical culmination of a series of events.

In environmental terms, in social terms, in terms of any one of a number of conventional measures and descriptions, the story of East Woodlawn is the story of all too many inner-city areas. The standard (and accurate) narrative is to refer to Woodlawn as a mile-square black ghetto on the south side of Chicago immediately to the south and adjacent to the University of Chicago. Its houses are substandard, its people poor. It has less than its share of jobs, income and vital services, and more than its share of dependence, dirt, disease, and early death. It has, in short, the full tangle of pathologies which chokes so many Negro neighborhoods and marks them off as slums. In large part these circumstances caused the city of Chicago and the Department of Housing and Urban Development in 1967 to designate Woodlawn the target area of the Mid-South Model Neighborhood Area.

A later section details the problems besetting Woodlawn and seeks to analyze these problems as the first step in a sequence of plan and program formulations which follows. However, there is an important "difference" which distinguishes Woodlawn and constitutes the ever-present backdrop to this entire document and to the process by which it was achieved.

The Woodlawn community has a voice; that voice combines the various points of view of active members of The Woodlawn Organization. It is the voice of Woodlawn—heard through T.W.O.—that has produced this Model Cities plan.

We have chosen our leaders, our officers, our staff, and our consultants in open and ongoing convocations

INTRODUCTION

from our 30,000-plus membership, drawing on our community's block groups, parents' councils, churches, social clubs, sub-area community organizations, social welfare unions, resident property owners, local businessmen, and, in large part, even the alienated youth. We do not rely on, as a matter of fact reject, the external selection of our community representatives, even when drawn from our midst, and contend that to proceed on this basis is to repeat, in a more sophisticated manner, the errors of the past and thus ensure certain programmatic failure. We ever seek to strengthen our democratic base through open and enlarging memberships functioning through committees, delegates' meetings, advisory boards, and annual conventions at which 2,000 or more are usually present.

We willingly accept our membership in the family of Chicago communities and recognize the merit of legislative review and approvals. However, we cannot (nor can any other community) assume our responsibilities and fulfill our obligations as a community member in the Chicago family unless we achieve the status of a full-fledged family member with the same range of choices available to other members.

The Woodlawn Organization

The "voice" of Woodlawn first began to be heard in 1960, when T.W.O. was formed. Out of a series of experiences, some bitter, with the University of Chicago and the city of Chicago, we learned two important lessons which formed the basis for a series of subsequent constructive activities and relationships:

(1) We discovered that we are citizens with rights

and with the latent power of all citizens if we assert our rights responsibly and systematically. Power can be an institution, a special interest group, a professional establishment, or a public agency, but it can also be people, banded together for a common cause, and with an articulate and recognizable voice.

(2) We perceived that it is not a public program per se which is the threat but rather its use. In the case of our initial confrontation with the city of Chicago and the University of Chicago, urban renewal was the feared instrument, but we satisfied ourselves that this instrument could be put into constructive service if fashioned to reflect the needs of the people now living in the community.

The Woodlawn Organization's planning effort grew and solidified, accompanied by a series of meetings with the University. We take note of these as another element culminating for us in this Model Cities plan. Faculty and students from the Department of Psychiatry, the Department of Pediatrics, the School of Education, and the Law School, among others, were interested in exploring with us how to fashion their respective professional performances into a cohesive community institution at both policy level and at delivery of services level. The University groups sought to enhance Woodlawn's ability to deploy professional functions and resources and thus strengthen its community decision-making capability. Each of the above University groups and others advanced "demonstration proposals" developed with The Woodlawn Organization covering concept and operation. Each of these activities had corollary public agency relationships, i.e., with the Board of

INTRODUCTION

CHART 1

**THE WOODLAWN ORGANIZATION STANDING COMMITTEES
AND
UNIVERSITY OF CHICAGO TASK FORCES**

T.W.O. STANDING COMMITTEE	UNIVERSITY OF CHICAGO TASK FORCES
SCHOOLS Chairman: Noel Alsbrook	EDUCATION Chairman: Prof. Roald Campbell
FINANCE (FUND-RAISING) Chairman: Worday Blair	EMPLOYMENT AND COMMERCIAL DEVELOPMENT Chairman: Prof. Robert McKersie
CONSUMER PRACTICES Chairman: Phyllis Hubbard	HEALTH Chairman: Dr. Robert S. Daniels Co-Chairmen: Dr. John D. Madden Dr. Sheppard G. Kellam Dr. Sheldon Schiff
HEALTH Chairman: Wiley Moore Co-Chairman: Brenda Coleman	
SOCIAL WELFARE Chairman: Jannie Nash President of Welfare Union: Annie Jackson	WELFARE AND FAMILY PLANNING Chairman: Asst. Prof. Harold A. Richman
CIVIL RIGHTS Chairman: E. "Duke" McNeill	LEGAL RIGHTS Chairman: Asst. Prof. Philip H. Ginsberg
HOUSING Chairmen: Andrew Smith Andrew Taylor Lee Langster	HOUSING AND ENVIRONMENTAL PLANNING Co-Chairmen: Prof. Brian J. L. Berry Prof. Julian H. Levi
WAYS AND MEANS Chairman: Rev. Arthur M. Brazier	CENTRAL TASK FORCE GROUP Co-Chairmen: Prof. Jack Meltzer Prof. Julian H. Levi
	OVER-ALL CONSULTATION Chairman: Prof. Morris Janowitz

Health, Board of Education, etc. What distinguished these demonstration programs from traditional efforts by governments and professions was that the community itself, through The Woodlawn Organization, the major community "voice," was involved at the outset and assumed a principal, responsible role in the planning, development, and implementation of them.

The continuing constructive activity of our Woodlawn Organization in connection with these University-associated projects, as well as other programs in a variety of fields, provided evidence that a black community with a voice can command the respect not only of its citizens but of the city and the academic community as well. The University professionals learned to order their operations, as well as their own professional requirements and habits, in terms of the desires and needs of the community as articulated by its citizens. The participants increasingly manifested their growing certainty that the only way to work in the community was in partnership with it, and that the only partnership that worked was for the University participant to assume the junior role.

**Model Cities Plan—
Organization and rocess**

The organizational skeleton of the work relationship followed T.W.O. committee structure. Certain of our committees were combined, and the following basic number were maintained throughout: Housing and Community Maintenance, Schools, Civil Rights, Consumer Practices and Finance, Social Welfare, and Health.

The University faculty and students organized themselves into counterpart task forces, following our struc-

INTRODUCTION

ture: Employment and Economic Development, Education, Health (physical and mental), Environmental Planning and Housing, Welfare and Family Planning, Legal, and Synthesis.

A Central Student Task Force was formed at the beginning of the summer to collect data, work with individual task forces, and help with the core responsibilities of putting the entire package together.

A large number of meetings convened in these connections during the summer: T.W.O. committees without the counterpart University group present, University committees without T.W.O. people present, and joint meetings of the above groups.

In addition, T.W.O. committee chairmen met together, as did University task force chairmen, to interrelate their respective efforts on an every-other-week basis. T.W.O. committee chairmen and task force chairmen met as an overall synthesis committee called the Ways and Means Committee.

The functional committees and task forces completed their individual report on Friday, September 27, 1968. These reports represented the output of the T.W.O. committee and reflected the technical input of the University task force.

The entire document was put together on Friday, October 4, 1968, and again reviewed by all our committees. A complete revision was made available to our T.W.O. 250-member planning council on Saturday, November 2, 1968. The changes sought by this group were incorporated. The document was then discussed at seven community-wide public hearings and by our 115 T.W.O. delegate organizations. The recommended changes growing out of these meetings are reflected in this document.

WOODLAWN'S MODEL CITIES PLAN

The process by which the document was prepared was full of stress and strain and reflected frequent abrasive meetings. While T.W.O. and the University people sought to develop creative and imaginative ideas, in a large number of cases they were dependent on certain crucial political decisions, reformulations of administrative systems and practices, profound adjustments in professional constitution, and the deployment of private and public financial resources. In many cases, the University faculty and students found it necessary to adapt their recommendations in the face of discussion with, and instructions from, our citizen committees. The process by which our Model Cities plan was prepared was exhilarating and difficult at the same time. Everyone's work load was tremendous, involving dozens of meetings and countless hours of preparation.

Three main dangers were involved. The first danger was that we, as well as the University professionals, would fall into what might be called "the comprehensiveness trap." In our zeal to identify every conceivable problem, trace each one to all its possible causes, and explore all possible remedies, we could well end up multiplying activities and compiling a kind of Sears, Roebuck catalogue. Were this to happen, all system would be lost, and we would have abandoned the "whole man" approach.

The second danger was that the Woodlawn-University partnership would fail to work the way it was intended. The advisors from the University might unconsciously our purposely "pull rank," overawe our citizens, and drive hard to secure our approval of plans which we did not devise or comprehend.

The third danger was that our citizens might "pull

INTRODUCTION

race" on the mostly white, middle-class University members, play upon their guilt feelings and self-consciousness, and force them to disregard facts or abandon sound judgments. One University personage, not deeply involved in the planning process, voiced fears of "chaos and anarchy" if the University paid too much heed to the community's opinions.

These dangers were not dismissed. They were addressed with frankness and candor by T.W.O. and the University people. And through the good faith and continuous exertions of citizens and experts, together, they were overcome.

To keep clear of "the comprehensiveness trap," The Woodlawn Organization and our University advisors attempted to look beyond the existing institutional structures and examine basic problem areas directly. The conventional thing to do would have been to adhere to traditional functional areas and then somehow seek to achieve coordination among them. But this approach, in our words, is just a "trick bag."

SUMMARY

The plan which follows is Woodlawn's own. Not only does it express the determination and the decisions of our community, but it reflects an understanding of neighborhood conditions that only neighborhood people have. Based on that understanding, it seeks to create an effective program which meets the standards established by the statute.

It offers new and imaginative proposals with substantial innovations in the nature of the program, in governmental cooperation, and in administration.

WOODLAWN'S MODEL CITIES PLAN

And in the process of planning, our community has demonstrated its commitment and its capacity to carry this program out.

By listening to the voice of the black community and approving this Model Cities plan, public authorities can acknowledge hope and reinforce dignity.

PROBLEM STATEMENT

WOODLAWN'S PROBLEMS: ROOT AND PROXIMATE CAUSES OF POVERTY

On all indices, Woodlawn ranks among the lowest of the seventy-six community areas of Chicago and is generally comparable to the twelve areas in Chicago that are defined as ghetto areas.

Rather than to document statistically the physical, economical, and social problems of Woodlawn (which are detailed in the Model Cities plan), it is of more relevance to identify the root cause of the conditions that are present in Woodlawn, as in other black ghettos. The segregation of the black American and the poverty in which he lives are inseparable sides of the same problem: a pervasive discrimination which has denied the Negro access to both the means and fruits of twentieth-century American affluence. And the urban Negro acutely feels that powerlessness which grows out of the discriminatory attitudes of the white majorities. He resents the "white power structure" which, he has come to believe, exploits him politically and economically: "Negroes . . . lack the channels of communication, influence, and appeal that traditionally have been available to ethnic minorities within the city and which enabled them—unburdened by color—to scale the walls of the white ghettos in an earlier era."[1] Yet racial prejudice is, in itself, insufficient to explain the cycle of poverty in which the Negro finds himself. Increasing urbanization and the changing structure of the economy are more proximate causes which must be balanced against the root cause of racism in an analysis of the problem.

Between 1910 and 1966, the number of Negroes living outside the south increased over five times as fast as the Negro population as a whole. Although Negro migration to northern cities began during the Civil War, it received considerable impetus during the two World Wars, which created numerous jobs in northern industrial plants. Increasing mechanization of agriculture in the south, combined with the promise of employment opportunities in the cities, explain a large part of the phenomenon of Negro migration. Negro urbanization has meant Negro segregation; in this respect Negroes are not dissimilar from other immigrant groups in the earlier part of the twentieth century who tended to live together in older sections of the central city, in proximity to cheap housing, sources of employment, friends, relatives, and countrymen. Unlike earlier immigrants, however, the Negro faces little prospect of breaking out of the ghetto; even where the Negro achieves some degree of economic success, he is unable to assimilate as have the members of previous immigrant groups, and must remain in predominantly Negro neighborhoods.

By 1960, for example, Chicago was experiencing a net annual out-migration of whites totaling 60,000 persons, nine-tenths of whom moved to the suburbs, and a net annual immigration of 15,000 to 16,000 non-whites. These rates have dropped off considerably since 1960; the city itself, for the first time in a century, appears to be decreasing in population as changing economic conditions, the second proximate cause which might be used to explain the endurance of the ghettos, increase the difficulty of absorbing a larger population in the central city.

PROBLEM STATEMENT

Sectoral shifts in the growth of the American economy during the postwar period have hit the Negro hard, first driving him out of the rural areas of the south into the metropolitan north and then hindering him from finding meaningful—indeed, often any—employment in the cities.

According to recent Labor Department projections of occupational growth trends in the economy, most blue-collar occupations are expected to experience lower rates of growth than the economy as a whole and, in the case of unskilled labor, virtual stagnation. Even under full-employment conditions, for example, it is expected that the number of unskilled industrial laborers in the country will remain at 1964 levels throughout the period 1964-1975. Automation, the replacement of labor by machinery, will largely be responsible for this stagnation. Semiskilled laborers, operatives, will experience similar, although not so severe, conditions of relative decline.

The city of Chicago has shared in these national trends. Initial analysis of an Illinois Department of Labor statewide survey of unemployed job seekers conducted jointly with Governor Otto Kerner's Committee on Unemployment reveals that "nearly two-thirds (66 per cent) of the jobless are in unskilled, semiskilled, and service occupations of which there is only limited demand in Chicago's labor market ... Approximately 40 per cent are Negroes. A breakdown of this group shows 81 per cent of them to be unskilled, semiskilled and service occupations ...."[2]

Chicago is experiencing additional economic shifts which reinforce these labor market trends on the employment of the Negro. Three of the major industries in the area which contributed in large part to the city's earlier growth have been seriously weakened in recent years: meat-packing, now performed closer to producing centers; steel, presently being eclipsed by such new production materials as aluminum; and railroads, an "empire which is slowly being taken over by truck and air transportation."[3] Since 1957 the overall employment trend in Chicago has been generally downward. Almost all sections of the city experienced job losses to a greater or lesser extent over the four-year period ending in mid-March, 1961. Chicago lost 139,000 jobs in this period. Firms moved from the city to the suburbs, as well as from one location to another within the city; some transferred to other sections of the country. Generally, the movement was from older congested areas to newer less congested locations.

The south side, including East Woodlawn and an area approximately from 3500 south to a line from 6700 to 7500 south and from 2400 west to the lake, lost 31,000 jobs, the second largest decrease in the city during the four-year period 1958-61. These trends apparently have continued to the present and reflect the area's continuing transition from white to Negro population. The portions of the city suffering the biggest reduction in employment were the most heavily blighted. Unemployment rates among Negroes in the area reflect these trends. The U.S. Census Bureau reported that, in 1959, while 3.8% of the male white labor force was without work, 10.8% of the male non-white population was unemployed in Chicago. In the East Woodlawn area in 1959, 12.2% of the male non-whites, or 1,666 out of 13,782 males in the civilian labor force, was without work. In other words, the unemployment rate for non-whites in East Woodlawn was more than three times as

PROBLEM STATEMENT

high as the rate for whites in Chicago. Nearly one out of eight employable male non-whites was out of work in East Woodlawn in 1959. This rate has risen over the past years, and overall unemployment in the area is currently estimated at 15% of the labor force—or almost one person out of every six.

A further shift in the American economy which adversely affects the mobility of the Negro relates to the decline of small businesses in recent years—an area which provided a major avenue of mobility to earlier immigrant groups. Brian J. L. Berry attributes the decline in retailing over the past fifteen years to three sorts of forces: changing buying habits fostered by rising real incomes and greater geographic mobility due to the automobile; social change in the central city, meaning the growth of Negro slums; and changing technology of retailing, in which increasing costs of labor relative to those of land and capital have hastened the rate at which businessmen have taken to larger scale, more automated forms of retailing. In addition, larger-scale, high-volume establishments can operate on slimmer margins, offering lower prices to cost-conscious consumers. This has meant powerful, often fatal competition for the smaller retailer, and the success of the larger stores in the new planned shopping centers and of discount houses. Applying Berry's statistical measures to East Woodlawn, now a low-income area that underwent transition during the forties and fifties, these figures portend a continuing decline in the number of business establishments at the geometric rate of 4% per year. One-half of all businesses in Woodlawn can expect to relocate every 2.1 years; one-half can expect to liquidate in twice that time. Thus, under present economic conditions, the Negro immigrant to the northern city cannot realistically hope to escape the ghetto through the historical avenue of small business ownership.

While present conditions in Woodlawn are symptoms of these and a variety of other basic and proximate causes of continuing Negro poverty, it is recognized that the root conditions cannot be attacked by Model Cities alone nor, indeed, any legislative fiat. No federal program can stem Negro migration to the cities; no law passed by Congress can reverse national secular trends in the economy. And, more significantly, laws cannot by themselves end racist feelings toward the black American. If the black man is to escape from ghetto living, he must alter those institutions which touch his daily life. In the first instance, black communities such as Woodlawn must develop a strong sense of community and achieve some measure of responsibility for those institutions which will largely determine their future. In the second instance, these institutions must reflect the realities of the community and the desires of its residents. The detailed Model Cities plan volume addresses these central issues.

SERVICE, HEALTH, AND EMPLOYMENT DEFICIENCIES

In considering service, health, and employment deficiencies, as identified and articulated by the citizens of Woodlawn, one must bear in mind the root conditions, previously elaborated, of which they are merely surface manifestations.

General Service Deficiencies, Including Financial Assistance

Basic services are generally available only through the

PROBLEM STATEMENT

welfare department—an agency understaffed by professional people, overburdened by financial priorities, and providing services only to those who are receiving public assistance. Those services which are offered have been determined by federal regulations rather than by community preference.

Aside from the lack of community resources outside of the welfare system, the few existing services directed to Woodlawn residents and located both within and outside the target area are poorly coordinated, and clients become lost in the process of referral.

The scarcity of essential social services in this community, as compared to other communities, is an abrogation of justice. Woodlawn is a community where one out of every ten men cannot find a job; where six out of ten high-school students drop out; and where one-quarter of the population is on welfare. Other statistics are equally depressing: its infant mortality rates, venereal disease rates, and premature birth rates are among the highest in the city. These conditions have been created and perpetuated by discrimination, neglect, and the endless denial of potential.

The need for access services is overwhelming. In a community where almost a quarter of the population receives public assistance, where the disease rates rank among the highest in the city, and where large segments of the population lack the necessary know-how to negotiate complex bureaucratic agencies, a lack of access means a lack of services.

Crisis intervention occurs more often at the convenience of agencies than in response to the needs of the people. The primary location for almost every social agency serving Woodlawn is on 63rd Street between

Cottage Grove and University Avenues, although over 75% of the population of the target area live south and east of this area. Very few agencies maintain evening hours, as if crises occurred only between the hours of nine and five.

Self-support services are totally inadequate in the face of a need which is evidenced by a male unemployment rate of 9% to 11%. The unemployment rate is much higher for teenagers and women.

Inadequate day-care services often undermine the effectiveness of self-support services. In 1966 there were 22,845 children in Woodlawn under the age of thirteen, of whom approximately 1,300 needed day-care services; yet it is almost impossible for women who are working or who have potential for self-support to find adequate day-care services. In all of Woodlawn there are spaces for only forty children in approved day-care facilities.

Inadequate incomes (in 1960, almost one-third of the population had an income of under $3,000, less than 7% had incomes of $10,000 or more) are further eroded by shortages of supermarkets, department stores, and discount houses. Instead, shopping is done at small neighborhood stores that offer second-rate merchandise at high prices. As in other low-income neighborhoods, door-to-door salesmen offer overpriced, shoddy merchandise "on convenient terms." Exorbitant interest rates must be paid by families who cannot pay cash or who cannot obtain credit at reputable stores. There are few avenues now open to the community through which these practices can be corrected or avoided.

The current level of financial assistance is too low to allow an adequate standard of living. The average grant

PROBLEM STATEMENT

level in Illinois is $2,544 per family of four, far less than the present poverty level in Chicago. A family receiving assistance in Illinois receives a monthly food allowance of $76.10, compared with the U.S. Department of Agriculture's low-cost monthly budget of $103.50 for the same size family. An allowance for furniture must be requested and then approved by the Department of Public Aid. Each family is allowed only one bed for every two persons, one chest of drawers per family, and a floor lamp if there is no other lighting in the room. The following items are not allowed: sofa, radio, television, clocks, rugs, and draperies.

The present financial assistance laws are designed to grant aid to as few people as possible. The categorical system of grants limits eligibility for financial assistance to several specific areas: the aged, the blind, the disabled, and dependent children and their parents. Those who are not in the above categories must rely on the vagaries of locally administered general assistance. Even within the above categories, an applicant for financial aid, because of the severe restrictions on personal property and income, must become a virtual pauper before receiving assistance.

Detailed and often demeaning investigations of eligibility for financial assistance reinforce and deepen feelings of despair and inadequacy of people who are in need. An application for public assistance is usually precipitated by an emotional as well as a financial crisis. Unemployment, old age, severe illness, or permanent disability may create feelings of hopelessness and dependency. A detailed investigation of eligibility consisting of one or more interviews in the person's home, questions unrelated to present need, and the demand for verification of every statement is not conducive to human dignity; this situation is worsened when the investigation is conducted in a hostile or punitive manner. By the time a person finally receives assistance, the feelings of degradation and shame evoked by the application process may have seriously impaired his chances of ever regaining self-respect or self-sufficiency.

Categorical distinctions in public assistance do not provide equal justice. The present system of establishing categories of assistance perpetuates the concept of worthy and unworthy poor. A family headed by an employed mother whose income is inadequate is eligible for assistance, while a family headed by a father in the same economic circumstances is not eligible. Need should be the sole eligibility requirement. Grants should be uniform and not based on arbitrary distinctions such as age or health.

Inadequate grants erode the self-respect and dignity of the recipient. A family in Illinois is allowed seventy-five cents per person per day for food. A family of ten is expected to find safe, adequate housing for $90 per month. A telephone is permitted only if a physician convinces the welfare department that a person's health transforms this item from a luxury to a necessity. A child on aid cannot join the Boy Scouts, engage in extracurricular school activities, or attend summer camp because these expenses are not allowed in the grant. A public assistance grant provides a basic subsistence allowance with no margin for error. Even legitimate "special needs" require proof and are subject to arbitrary decisions made by the agency. An inadequate diet; an overcrowded, substandard apartment; and insufficient clothing are constant reminders not only of

PROBLEM STATEMENT

poverty but of society's censure of those whom it considers unproductive. The President's Advisory Committee on Public Assistance has stated unequivocally that the government is one of the chief contributors to the continuing poverty upon which it has declared an unconditional war.

Health Deficiencies

As one examines the usual indices of morbidity and mortality, East Woodlawn emerges as having one of the highest rates in the city. Statistics provided by the 1964 Community Area Profile show that Woodlawn ranks seventy-second among seventy-five communities on six health measures. These include percentages of premature births, syphilis, gonorrhea, tuberculosis, congenital malformation, and poisoning. For example, in mortality rates per 1,000 population, Woodlawn rates are consistently 1.5 to 3 times as high as the city as a whole; similar figures are found for typical morbidity rates. Maternal mortality, prematurity, prenatal mortality, illegitimacy, mental illness, school maladaptation, and delinquency all confirm this statement. Only two of the seventy-six community areas had higher venereal disease rates in 1960. An overburdened, inadequate health system has no resources with which to plan and implement adequate early detection systems. Maladaptation is usual. Rehabilitation—physical, social, or emotional—is rare.

The lack of adequate physician manpower in the Woodlawn area—typical of the general, increasing shortages of health personnel—is apparent in a study on physician availability in Woodlawn. The 1952 neighborhood telephone directory listed forty-six physicians with offices in East Woodlawn. By 1962 the number had declined to twenty-nine. Recent informal surveys suggest that more than 20% of these physicians are in specialty practice and, therefore, do mainly referral work. A number have second offices and spend only part of their time in Woodlawn. Many see no more than 35% of their patients from the Woodlawn area. Of the group still practicing in Woodlawn, the average age is close to sixty and only one is under forty. Three are over eighty. In terms of full-time physician equivalents, there are certainly no more than twenty, an average of 1:3,000 residents, only about 25% of the national average.

Hospital care is offered in a variety of places, mainly outside of Woodlawn and nearby areas. About 50% of hospital care occurs at Cook County Hospital, approximately ten miles away by direct transportation or an hour by public transportation. In the East Woodlawn area there is a single private, not-for-profit community hospital. Four other hospitals are no more than three-quarters of a mile away. Totally their capacity is approximately 1,700 beds. In the 1965 Hospital Planning Council study, Woodlawn residents occupied about 7% of their beds. A recent study of two local hospitals, Woodlawn Hospital and the University of Chicago Hospitals, suggested that there has been some change in the last three years. Currently, more than 16% of the patients hospitalized at Woodlawn Hospital come from Woodlawn. The comparable percentage for the University of Chicago Hospitals is approximately 12%. Despite these significant increases, Woodlawn residents are most often hospitalized in distant places. Cook County Hospital continues to be the largest single provider of hospital services.

PROBLEM STATEMENT

The financing of medical services continues to be a problem. The complexities of registration and screening discourage many eligible individuals from applying. Although public welfare, Medicare, and Medicaid have been helpful in funding, large populations continue to be medically indigent. Often they are not defined as eligible under current regulations. As a result, these individuals either are not served, or, if they are, served at a loss to the agency or institution providing the service. Currently, the Illinois Department of Public Aid is as much as two years behind in its payments to institutions and physicians. Another major problem has been the difficulty in providing continuing services irrespective of income. Either only certain target populations are eligible, thus resulting in fragmentation of family medical care, or a changed income makes it impossible to continue within the same system. Only limited attention has been given either locally or nationally to combining systems of public funding with prepaid comprehensive care. Even more unusual is the possibility for flexibly moving from one system of payment to another without disruption or change in health providers or services.

Current local experiences in health-care systems suggest that only about a third of populations residing in communities like Woodlawn are covered through public sources. Another third have third-party coverage to finance their own health care. The third in between, however, cannot pay for their own health needs and there are limited or no sources for reimbursement currently available.

WOODLAWN'S MODEL CITIES PLAN

Employment Deficiencies

Unemployment is high in Woodlawn. Approximately 15% of the work force can be counted as unemployed. This amounts to some 4,700 individuals. The teenage and young worker categories with unemployment rates of at least 30% and 20%, respectively, account for approximately half, or 2,300, unemployed individuals. Many adults in Woodlawn are not included in the above figures because they are not able to look for work, and hence are not counted in the labor force. For example, many mothers would be interested in employment if facilities were available for the care of their children.

Underutilization of employed workers is the other side of the problem of high unemployment. Approximately 25% to 30% more workers fall in the laboring and service occupations than is true for the citywide profile. If this disparity could be eliminated, approximately 8,700 workers would stand to be upgraded.

Existing Manpower Program Deficiencies

In taking inventory of the programs already on the scene, it is clear that considerable activity has occurred in preparing hard-core individuals for employment and facilitating their placement in job openings available throughout the city. The Illinois State Employment Service (ISES) operates an office on 63rd Street (as part of the Urban Progress Center); various Manpower Development and Training Act (MDTA) programs have been in existence for the past several years; several Office of Economic Opportunity (OEO) programs such

PROBLEM STATEMENT

as the Neighborhood Youth Corps (NYC) have attempted to work with the hard-core; and T.W.O. has operated numerous programs such as the Youth Training Project and others under contract with the U. S. Department of Labor.

But important gaps are still present in the worker preparation field:

(1) Intensive contact and follow-through of the hard-core is lacking. The ISES provides the valuable function of referring individuals to agency programs and to job openings throughout the city, but it is not in a position to provide counseling or followup work for individuals who need high support.

(2) Clientele-related job development has not taken place. A tremendous gap exists at present between the development of openings and the preparation of individuals. What is needed is a matching of these two functions by a new agency at the local level in Woodlawn. Such an agency might do the following: (a) contact companies and other employing institutions and secure employment contracts for Woodlawn workers (in some cases it would be necessary to revise the hiring standards and otherwise to tailor the employment arrangements to the specific clientele); and (b) enroll individuals in the proper training and orientation programs in order to qualify them for the specific job opportunities. Thus far, T.W.O. has engaged in a modest amount of this type of "advocate" job and worker preparation.

(3) Little connection has occurred between the learning and earning phases of a person's career. The dropout rate at Hyde Park High School remains high: in the vicinity of 30%-35%. And for those already beyond the normal school age, the amount of formal education

possessed is small. Only one-third of Woodlawn residents hold high-school diplomas; this group could benefit from basic education and vocational training. Specific skill-training programs are important but they will enable individuals only to get started in industry, whereas basic education would prepare them for career progression and not isolation in dead-end jobs.

Additional Economic Deficiencies

Additional economic difficulties that beset the Woodlawn community include job inaccessibility, lack of job opportunities within the community, lack of community equity (black entrepreneurship), and income drainage.

Job Inaccessibility. Very few of the 31,000 members of the Woodlawn labor force are employed in or near the community. It has been estimated that approximately 2,300 individuals work in the business establishments in Woodlawn, most of these being retail stores. Another 200-300 individuals work at the University of Chicago. In general, probably no more than 3,000 individuals work within walking distance of the Woodlawn residential area.

Lack of Local Job Opportunities. To date, very little activity has occurred on the job-creation side of the employment picture. Except for the few jobs which will be created by the new developments on Cottage Grove Avenue, very little attention has been given to the attraction of new industry into the area. Some T.W.O. staff members have talked with large Chicago companies about the possibility of locating plants in the Woodlawn area, but

PROBLEM STATEMENT

little has resulted from these probes. The Chicago Economic Development Corporation (CEDC), which has an office on 63rd Street, has devoted some of its energies to this subject but has thus far been unsuccessful.

While the task of attracting new industry into Woodlawn is formidable, most of the ingredients of success are present: several parcels of land, transportation arrangements for in-product and finished-product movement, an ample labor supply, and financial resources (through the Small Business Administration (SBA) or local banks such as the Hyde Park Bank, which has established an urban development division for this purpose) are all available. The main gap is the absence of an organization to put the pieces of industrial expansion together. Some type of housing and economic development corporation could provide the sponsorship and impetus for an industrial park and for the generation of other business ventures in Woodlawn, especially along 63rd Street

Black Entrepreneurship. Very few of the economic units in Woodlawn are owned by residents. Approximately 25% of the homes are owner-occupied and no more than 5%-10% of the 500 retail and service businesses are owned and operated by Woodlawn residents.

In addition, another 100—120 small manufacturing, transportation, and construction firms are located in Woodlawn, but virtually none of these is operated by residents.

Many individuals in Woodlawn have expressed a strong desire to go into business for themselves. The local CEDC office has received numerous inquiries. At the meetings held with Woodlawn residents about economic development, inevitably the discussion turned to the favorite subject of many individuals, "Why can't I start my own business?"

While it is certainly true that many individuals are not suited to become entrepreneurs and that many existing businesses in Woodlawn are not viable business opportunities (given the high mortality), a situation of little black ownership and a substantial desire on the part of residents to own their own enterprises is one that calls for a program—specifically, a small business development center.

Income Drainage. It is estimated that between 90% and 95% of income spent by residents of Woodlawn drains from the community. Over one-quarter of Woodlawn income is spent in stores located within the community; the total "feedback" into Woodlawn, in the form of profits to resident merchants and wages to resident employees, amounts to some 14% of this amount—less than 4% of area income. An additional 15% drains to rental payments to landlords who live outside the community; a substantial part of this drain can be attributed to rent differentials between black and white tenants in Woodlawn (whites rentals average 78% of Negro rentals in the community), amounting to almost 3% of the total income of the area—some $5.4 million yearly. Put somewhat differently, if rentals paid by Negroes were reduced to the levels paid by whites in Woodlawn, the "savings" to the community would be greater than those which would be realized were all the local stores owned by area residents who retained their profits within the community ("drain" to profits of nonresident merchants with stores in Woodlawn is estimated at only $4 million, some 2% of total area income).

While business ownership by residents may not be

PROBLEM STATEMENT

important from an economic point of view, the psychological value of having residents in positions of economic leadership nevertheless could be very considerable.

There is need for new, possibly cooperative institutions to provide essential services and to enable the residents to participate in important economic areas. For example, many residents have indicated that insurance and credit are areas where inadequate services are being offered.

OTHER DEFICIENCIES

Multiple Administrative Districts

Critical deficiencies exist in connection with education, legal services, recreation, and housing. An overall deficiency in the Woodlawn community is the lack of unified boundaries defining different functional districts such as education, health, welfare, etc. A reconstitution of boundary divisions along community lines would be valuable for the following reasons:

(1) Administration of community needs would be facilitated by placing agency purview territorially within the community.

(2) Shared responsibility among all agencies, for purposes of planning and service delivery, is possible only if all agencies have responsibility for servicing the same constituency.

(3) Assessment of community need requires a common denominator for all agencies; evaluation of programs requires that all agencies measure along the same base.

(4) Capacity for agency receptivity to community needs depends on its responsibility: if an agency's performance

is judged on the basis of its response to the needs of its constituency, it is more likely to perform effectively for the citizens of any given community when those citizens comprise its sole constituency and, hence, the sole basis for evaluation of the agency's performance.

Footnotes

[1] **Report of the National Advisory Commission on Civil Disorders,** New York: New York Times Company, 1968, p. 205.

[2] ISES, "Chicago Area Labor Market Trends," Vol. XVIII, No. 2 (Cal. 1962).

[3] Pierre de Vise, **Chicago's Widening Color Gap,** the Inter-University Social Research Committee, December, 1967, p. 2.

GOALS, OBJECTIVES, AND STRATEGIES: THE BASIC FRAMEWORK OF THE MODEL CITIES PLAN

HOW THE PLAN IS CONSTITUTED

The problems of an inner-city community such as Woodlawn tend to overwhelm not only its residents but analysts as well. In consequence, "total" approaches are often brought into play to deal with "total" frustration. The result of this is too often an incomprehensible array of projects which fails to produce anything but discouragement among the residents, largely because the "total" approach demands administration and "coordination" on a scale that is simply unworkable and unattainable.

The Model Cities instrument may lead the unwary into this trap since following HUD guidelines could result in a recitation, at length and in breadth, of every conceivable factor, goal, purpose, and function related to the target area. The governing principle then becomes "comprehensiveness," for if we do not know the cause of problems or any specific remedies for them the wisest course is to respond massively, trusting that somehow benefit will filter down through the expanded, established administration and bureaucracy.

The approach of the Woodlawn community to Model Cities planning has meticulously guarded against being merely "comprehensive" and has focused rather on a process involving specific problem diagnosis and goal determination, selective programmatic treatment, and continuous assessment of goal achievement in all programs.

WOODLAWN'S MODEL CITIES PLAN

This approach is consistent with and reinforces the individual and family orientation of the Woodlawn Model Cities effort. A "comprehensive" approach lends itself too easily to a self-serving professional orientation in which activities are expanded additively into a jumbled aggregate which follows and is "organized" along traditional professional lines.

We have labored to avoid the prevalent pattern of merely extending vertically the established professional functions (health, welfare, social service, etc.)—a practice which generally proceeds with little relation to problems as perceived by the individuals and families whom these functions are intended to serve.

Consequently, although the Woodlawn community has been examined by its residents and their University consultants, as a whole, the program recommendations advanced below constitute no attempt to "coordinate established services" based on the principle of "comprehensiveness," but a deliberate and systematic strategy of response to the problems and functions fragmenting Woodlawn.

The recommendations constitute a highly selective set of specifically articulated activities, flowing from an identified series of critical goals dictated by and related to perceived problems. While the criteria and goals which guided this plan's formulation are specified later, the selected activities in the proposed undertaking were developed to achieve a wide range of collateral purposes.

The recommended activities, in other words, are the keys which unlock the doors to the realization of a wide range of diverse aims and objectives. The plan assumes that the proper linkage would be achieved through an inventive process of creating new operating relationships which would flow from a unified system of planning and programming, a set of mutually agreed upon goals and a new organizing principle. The proposed plan relies only minimally on the "coordination" of diverse activities, each with its own private goal, each independently planned, and each reporting to a different city, county, or state government, or to a different national agency.

Thus, while the Woodlawn Model Cities plan does not seek to diminish the social and political responsibility which devolves on the city, county, and state in connection with the problems of the inner city, the needs of the plan (and a major premise underlying it) require that the functional agencies associated with each of these levels of government be ready to (1) modify their organizational arrangements and lines of authority where they touch Woodlawn, and (2) reconcile and make consistent the jurisdictional boundaries of their administrative subdivisions. At present, each functional agency has its own administratively defined district which contradicts all the others, a situation which produces confusion and bureaucratic redundancy, hides information, hamstrings research, and, generally, prevents the people from being adequately served.

Finally, professional agencies must acquire programmatic and administrative flexibility to respond to old and new problems. The lack of such flexibility is now so blatant that existing "service agencies" constitute major community problems in their own rights.

Flexibility is critical to the Woodlawn Model Cities plan, since it is a highly selective combination of program components. The plan requires continuous evaluation in which program results are tested against the rate and degree to which they are contributing to goal achievement. Unsatisfactory rates of change may require program redirection or new program combinations. Evaluation thus becomes a program management instrument as well as a means for gathering data and assessing performance. But this evaluation is pointless if it is not used to modify the ongoing programs where and when required, a process dependent on institutional flexibility.

OPERATIONAL MEASURES

We have sought to delimit major areas of need and present alternative objectives relating to the satisfaction of those needs. Important to this process is an evaluation component geared to the development of specific measures against which program success or failure can be assessed. While recognizing the utility of such measures, we felt that specific operational measures related to the programs herein proposed must await implementation of those programs before they can be meaningfully specified. Only in this fashion can measures serve as a bridge between evaluation, goals and objectives, and specific program approaches.

In developing these measures an analytic distinction will be made between two sorts of measures: those that refer to "input targets" and those that refer to "output targets." The first provide a measure of "program performance," focusing on specific program inputs. For example, one such measure might be the ratio of students to teachers, evaluated on the basis of a target set equal to some hypothetically ideal ratio (such as the ratio that currently obtains in nonghetto Chicago communities). The second provides a measure of "system performance," focusing on overall program outputs. An example might be an index of student maladaption to

GOALS, OBJECTIVES AND STRATEGIES

school, based on a set of such variables as report card, teacher assessment, delinquent behavior, etc. This would indicate the impact of various Model Cities programs, acting in concert, upon the residents of the community.

Once in operation, these performance measures would fall into place within the evaluation framework developed; specific measures then can be drawn from among those identified in the Model Cities plan, consistent with the measurement of program performance on the one hand and system performance on the other. Additional measures could be then devised as necessary, thereby constituting a sensitive barometric management tool which would permit the achievement of an optimal balance between input and output and between program and system. In this context, inputs are viewed as resources to be deployed, e.g., numbers of teachers, classrooms, etc., and outputs are viewed as the evidences of programmatic achievement, i.e., as a reflection of the wisdom utilized in the deployment of these resources.

GOALS AND OBJECTIVES

To overcome the complex of problems faced by Woodlawn and to effect citizen responsibility, Woodlawn residents have formulated a series of goals for Model Cities planning in their community. These goals are broad enough and high enough so that, when achieved, they would exceed achievement standards in statutory areas of concern and markedly improve the quality of life in Woodlawn.

There are four central, ordering goals. The first three goals given below reflect the major problems crippling the community, and indicate who suffers most: the young, the unemployed, and others who are variously incapacitated. The fourth goal derives from the ordering principles and the conditions facing the community, and provides a specific, continuous yardstick for measuring change and the achievement of the community's values. The first three goals indicate the key programs which are the central means for the realization of success, and the fourth refers to those specific physical forms in which the living processes of the community are concretized: the long-run improvement of the quality of housing and common community facilities.

They cover, in sequence, the educational process, employment opportunity, income levels, and housing and environmental conditions, thereby touching every stage of Woodlawn residents' lives. To specify the concern further:

(1) Education of the young, including new opportunities for education outside of the school. This constitutes the central goal for the undertaking because it sets in motion the processes of long-term self-revitalizing of the community.

(2) Employment, however, represents a coordinate focus because it emphasizes both long-range economic development and the more immediate objective of dealing with the large number of unemployed young adults.

(3) Income maintenance and social services, in turn, provide the financial and social assistance needed by those persons who by reason of physical or social disability or family responsibility find themselves without necessary resources.

(4) A decent home and a suitable living environment for every family remain unachieved in Woodlawn. The program undertaken to achieve the first three goals

ultimately must be evaluated largely by its ability to fulfill this unkept promise.

All program components, within the aegis of each of the professional functional groups (health, social service, law and others), would be shaped to achieve these ends and would be assessed according to the degree to which they reinforce these purposes. These stated goals and objectives would constitute a statement of priorities when specific resources are allocated and would be the basis for influencing the character of all constituent program elements in health, welfare, social service, law, and other fields.

STRATEGY

Overall Strategic Considerations

Model Cities guidelines refer to citizen participation as a necessary standard among and along with a series of twenty-two other equally necessary program standards. This leaves unsettled whether what is intended by citizen participation is deferential involvement, formal plan concurrence (to avoid the alternative of active citizen opposition), broad-scale representation as acceptable proof of participation (even if unaccompanied by step-by-step involvement), or any one of a number of other possible variations.

But no matter. This Woodlawn Model Cities plan views citizen involvement as the prime ingredient at every stage of the undertaking. This plan represents its product and constitutes the underlying necessity throughout the implementation phase. The plan takes "involvement" to mean a formal and acknowledged role for the citizen in the decision-making and implementing process, sanctioned by the community residents, the city of Chicago, and the federal government. The claim is asserted forcefully that the program recommendations lose a substantial part of their validity if the community role in overseeing the undertakings is diminished. Faced with a choice, a greater benefit would accrue in modifying the scale of the proposals than in limiting or curtailing the community role and influence. More appropriate to our Woodlawn Model Cities conception is "citizen responsibility" rather than either the phrase citizen participation or citizen involvement.

"Citizen responsibility," the first major principle underlying this plan, establishes both the spirit and the frame of the Woodlawn Model Cities package and contributes to each of the program proposals at both policy and operational levels (via a heavy reliance on nonprofessionals).

This issue takes on paramount importance for a number of reasons. First, we are convinced that major citizen responsibility is at the very center of inner-city problem resolution. No less significant, we view citizen responsibility as the key to individual motivation to avail oneself of the program opportunities provided by the Model Cities effort and to make the most of such opportunities. And, of considerable importance, citizen responsibility provides the means to internalize confrontation *within* an established legal system as opposed to externalizing conflict and thus constituting a threat to the system.

The second major principle is that program instruments would be modified to enable recipients of public aid and assistance to perform as consumers—in welfare, housing, employment, and the like—so as to reduce and ultimately to eliminate the current dependence of recipients on various public agencies. Hence income maintenance programs are preferable to welfare budgets, rent supplements to public housing construction, health insurance programs to philanthropic clinics, and so forth.

The third major principle cutting across the Woodlawn Model Cities plan is that wherever the option exists, or can be nurtured in all cases where the opportunity can be created, nonprofessionals and semiprofessionals would be engaged to perform tasks heretofore reserved for professionals. This would be done not solely as the means of husbanding limited professional resources, but also as an affirmative extension of the principle of "citizen responsibility."

The framework established here is not advanced with the claim that, if implemented, controversy thereby would be avoided. As a matter of fact, the events of the last few years have made clear that increased power by a growing number of groups tends to multiply the instances of confrontation.

What is claimed is that the proposed framework would increase the probabilities of accommodation and provide a systematic means to deal with controversy by making it possible to resolve differences within a sanctioned and rational institutionalized arrangement.

Realistic Model Cities planning requires a capacity to deal with evidences of program disappointments and even failure. In large part this is dealt with (and discussed) in connection with the means by which program components and combinations are realigned and refashioned in the face of the degree of goal achievement during the course of the undertaking.

Program success may have certain consequences, however, since controversy often results when one group's expectations (and its satisfaction) requires accommodation to, or sharply challenges, another group's behavior, i.e., when the Model Cities universe encounters the larger urban universe.

A major ancillary function of both the Core and the outreach facility (the Pad), discussed later, is a capacity for crisis forecasting; i.e., the sensitivity and ability to determine that conditions and attitudes exist in such combination as to require immediate response by the existing institutions and organizations and warrant attention at either the Model Cities, total city, or metropolitan level.

Strategic Framework

Three systems are proposed to realize the stated principles and goals: (1) a Core and outreach system, (2) an educational system, and (3) a housing and economic development corporation (including employment and training).

The Core and Outreach System: The Core

The Core is the central means by which the Woodlawn community will assert responsible citizenship. The Core will be a not-for-profit community public corporation with membership open to Woodlawn residents without cost. The corporation is a response to the need for a legally-constituted mechanism through which the

GOALS, OBJECTIVES AND STRATEGIES

community can deal with agencies and departments at all levels of government and with private parties to advance the community's interests. The community corporation will be authorized to receive public and private funds, to contract for public and private services, to own and/or operate facilities, to expend funds in Woodlawn's community interest after prescribed legal actions, to create and operate privately and publicly subscribed health and social service insurance programs, to review and approve budgets related to Core functions, and to oversee and interrelate the component program elements (discussed later as is the Core's organizational structure).

The deployment of program resources in the interests of achieving the highest degree of program integration constitutes a major purpose, e.g., vocational training within the aegis of the school, clearly bearing a close relationship to employment and economic development; health to schooling and employment; etc. It is in the Core that the traditional professional fields will be concentrated and the professional backup facilities to the outreach facilities will be housed. However, even within these professional backup facilities, nonprofessionals will be utilized on a wide-ranging basis. The principal functional groupings in the Core include health and social service (excluding hospitals, nursing homes, and convalescent homes which will be separately consolidated organizationally); financial services (income maintenance, independent of social services); environmental planning; and legal services (each of these is discussed later). These functions, currently encompassed within larger functional systems, would be refashioned and operate within the above-described framework. The operating heads of the Housing and Economic Development Corporation (HED) and the Woodlawn Community Board for Urban Education Projects (WCB)[1] responsible for the education system would maintain dual relationships within the Core organization.

City services (police, fire, public works, housekeeping, building code enforcement, etc.) would continue to be provided by the city of Chicago—subject, however, to certain defined community review functions discussed in connection with the legal service component. It is not possible or desirable for a Model Cities proposal to envisage local control over citywide or statewide functions of established agencies. Proper financing of Woodlawn schools requires recourse to the total tax base of Chicago, the Board of Education, and state aid resources, as well as to federal assistance. The legally determined duties of these agencies and departments make it impossible for a single community to wrest control from them, and Woodlawn in no manner wishes to imply that this is any part of the community's intention. The community has no desire to oust the Cook County Department of Public Aid, the Board of Education, or any state agency from overall control and line functions: their legal authority, personnel, funds and skills are desperately needed—and not only by Woodlawn—although they must develop more flexibility and responsiveness to the individual problems and situations of particular communities. All that Woodlawn is seeking is the provision of established mechanisms for accomplishing this latter necessity.

A board will be created to oversee the Core operation and will in turn select an executive, designated the convenor. The board will consist of one hundred residents of the Greater Woodlawn area. This area is defined as bounded by East 60th Street on the north;

GOALS, OBJECTIVES AND STRATEGIES

East 75th Street on the south; Stony Island Avenue on the east; and an irregular line on the west from a point at Martin Luther King Drive and East 60th Street thence south to 67th Street, thence eastward along South Chicago Avenue to 71st Street, eastward on 71st Street to the Illinois Central Railroad tracks, and thence south to 75th Street.

Forty of the one hundred board members will be elected at large for a three-year period. Nominations for each of these forty positions will be by petition signed by one hundred residents of Woodlawn, eighteen years of age and over. The at-large election will be conducted under the supervision of a nationally recognized organization with experience in conducting such elections.

The remaining sixty board members will be elected by the T.W.O. delegates meeting from a slate of nominees proposed as follows: one candidate will be nominated from each of the member organizations; of these nominees, sixty organizational members will be elected.

It should be re-emphasized that T.W.O. is a community organization open for membership and participation to all residents of the Greater Woodlawn community.

The board will elect twenty from their number as an executive committee. Twelve members of this committee will be chosen from the sixty board members elected from the organizational nominees; the other eight will come from the forty members elected at large.

Office of the Community Convenor. The office and person of the community convenor are conceived as the most promising form to achieve the desired goals. Just as Congress and the President induce needed collaboration at a very high level, the principles that led to that combination of efforts need to be carried out at a local level. In fact, the philosophy and commitment of the President and the Congress practically require this kind of strategy if there is to be any chance of success. The convenor concept recommended here is predicated on the precedent established by the President of the United States in Executive Order 11297, dated August 11 and August 13, 1966 (copy included in the detailed Model Cities plan volume). The convenor will fulfill the objective of responsible community control over its own affairs and, therefore, must be able to modify, or cause the agencies themselves to modify, the inherited patterns of practices that affect the community. In addition to being charged with dealing with outside forces affecting the community, the convenor will be responsible to the community board and report regularly to them and their chairman. Further, the relation of the convenor and the governing board must be dependent on the closest possible cooperation, since the responsibilities of the governing board will be made meaningless and empty unless the convenor has the power to ensure that the principles of the community are being carried out: for instance, that the operations of the Pads system is accomplishing the particular realization of those principles at the most personal and local level.

The duties of the community convenor can be summarized in the following four points. He:

(1) Ensures the complementary operation of the various community corporations, systems, boards, and programs.

(2) With approval of the governing board's executive committee, controls allocation of the city's pro-rata assign-

ments to Woodlawn of the federal 80% of Model Cities matching funds, including allocations to the Core, the Pads, the HED, and the WCB.

(3) Heads the Core organizational structure and bears ultimate executive responsibility for its operations. The convenor will enforce the personal guidelines of Woodlawn's Model Cities plan throughout the Core and Outreach systems to ensure the employment of the maximum number of community people.

(4) Is responsible directly and via the executive committee to the corporation governing board on budget, program, personnel and all other matters.

To ensure, on the one hand, that the convenor is provided an adequate period of security, he will be engaged for three-year terms upon majority vote of the governing board duly convened; to guarantee, on the other hand, a measure of final governing board control, he may be removed at any time during the three-year term upon two-thirds vote of the governing board duly convened.

The convenor, in addition to overseeing the functions referred to above, also has available to him special staff units dealing with plan and program formulation; information, data collection, and research; budget review; and evaluation. These functions require elaboration as follows:

Evaluation: A staff function of the convenor that will constitute a major management and programming tool, evaluation is keyed to the systematic translation of goals into performance standards and, in turn, into measurable criteria.

This approach stands in contrast to the strongly held view (shared by the city of Chicago in its Model Cities planning) that a survey, which asks people what they want or the selection of a supposedly diversely representative group who will express and thereby reflect what the people want, is the means of establishing the degree of citizen satisfaction. This is a white middle-class assumption which has little validity in an inner-city area. Such methods may have validity where community and citywide institutions exist which constitute and exercise power in the decision-making process. The survey technique and the "representative council" devices, therefore, provide useful means to establish precise goals and purposes which have been established and sanctioned institutionally and to select among and refine qualitative differences in a population with a range of choice.

In an inner city, choice is not provided by solitary reliance on either of these methods. To go back to offices and drawing boards after completing a survey or visiting with the "diversely representative group" is to engage in an exercise which leaves the visited population with an unchanged sense of frustration.

A prior step is required to set in motion a process of involvement and thereby create a climate in which attitudes are formed that cause people to begin to feel that problems can and will be solved over time and their aspirations thus fulfilled. The primary requirements are to facilitate the sense of community, strengthen existing organizations and institutions, and aid in establishing new community institutions where they do not exist. This is the strongest basis for working through already established, as well as embryonic, local organizations and institutions. Survey instruments and "representative" groups can then begin to play a useful role.

GOALS, OBJECTIVES AND STRATEGIES

Information, Data Gathering, and Research: We are proposing an ongoing statistical, research, and analysis effort which would report on the social and economic "health" of Woodlawn and have later applicability to all of Chicago's local communities and to subregions in the metropolitan area outside of Chicago. Initially for Woodlawn, and ultimately for all of Chicago, the program will result in a barometer of community well-being. It will incorporate an assessment of the rate and character of change as measured against identifiable indices and criteria.

In view of the current interest in "social accounting" and the recognition of the importance of social factors in environmental planning, we believe that both the results of this proposal and the research methods used in it will constitute important scientific contributions. The testimony on "The Full Opportunity and Social Accounting Acts of 1967" before the Subcommittee on Government Research of the Senate Committee on Government Operations documents the immediate need for developing a system of "social accounting" that could result in the publication of a President's "Social Report" paralleling the President's "Economic Report." This is no less essential at the local level where there is needed also a qualitative basis for policy formulation and program administration for both economic and social problems. This proposal provides the opportunity to develop local applications of this approach, building on the Woodlawn Model Cities exposure, and to extend the *Community Fact Book* which has so well served the Chicago area for decades.

The theme of the Model Cities program, "to improve the quality of urban life," indicates the importance of the social contribution to the success of the program. The achievement of the Model Cities objective, in the final analysis, depends on the recognition, analysis, and treatment of relevant social factors. Yet compared with the tools of economic analysis which are being utilized, indicators of social maladies which would relate to both cause and cure are in a very crude stage of development.

The past reliance on gross statistical sources has diminished our social planning capacity. The need exists to explore new data sources and to experiment with new data retrieval systems which could serve the variety of agencies interested in urban problems. Planning for Woodlawn's Model Cities Plan proceeded on the basis of required descriptions of social, economic, and physical factors in the target area drawn from traditional data found in census reports and similar health and welfare enumerations. This type of data barely covers the surface problems of the communities which are slated to undergo massive social restructuring. An improvement in the quality of community descriptions and analyses would enable planners to better understand and anticipate the inputs and outputs of community rebuilding.

Over and above the difficulties in grasping the complex makeup of the Woodlawn target area, means are available for more sensitive and systematic characterization of Woodlawn (as well as other communities) and for the identification of basic relationships. Through probing the more subtle characteristics of the community, we can extend and refine our community delineations and provide planners with criteria for community definition that will contribute to program effectiveness rather than remain simply geographic descriptions.

In addition, substantial public community involvement and expenditures provide an important added dimension

GOALS, OBJECTIVES AND STRATEGIES

requiring quantification and assessment. In-depth before, interim, and after surveys of the type envisioned in this proposal would provide information vitally important in assessing and evaluating progress and improving the impact of expenditures.

To achieve these purposes we must:

(1) Extend the current statistical examination of Woodlawn, which mainly recapitulates census materials, to include statistical information on factors outside of the census, including the incorporation of new data retrieval systems and the use of school, voting, crime and delinquency, health, welfare, housing, building code, etc. data. Since 1960 great strides have been achieved in the collection and use of non-census materials. These need to be tapped and organized systematically.

(2) Emphasize qualitative and quantitative materials which highlight growth and change and the impact of intervening public and private programs with a view to developing tension indices through supplementary field surveys and interviews.

(3) Collect basic data on institutions and organizations and their roles and functions in the social and economic structures of communities.

(4) Reexamine the neighborhood and community delineations which provide the basis for public and private activity.

The rationale underlying this proposal for the Woodlawn Model Cities area is to create (1) an instrument responsive to the changing requirements of "social accounting," and (2) a mechanism to assess public and private policy impact by ventilating the character and direction of community change.

Planning and Programming: The planning and programming staff function attached to the convenor within the Core is the critical device for continuous examination of the component elements which comprise the program package. It is the means for achieving "horizontal program" involvement cutting across functions in lieu of the earlier discussed conventional pattern of expanding functions vertically.

Modeling may constitute a scientific instrument to aid the planning and programming function. It is an instrument which permits the replication of reality by a process approximating a laboratory setting, conceptually and scientifically, and thereby make manageable both comprehension and complex programming. To date "modeling" has been limited to functional areas—most notably the transportation and health systems, although some modest beginnings have been made in modeling the urban system.

What is suggested here is a pioneering effort in the use of a model which would focus on the Woodlawn resident and the Woodlawn community in terms of characteristics, problems and needs, goals and aspirations; and which then would place Woodlawn within the total city and metropolitan context, with a view to identifying (1) the required resources, avenues to access, and other dependency relationships, as well as available opportunities for problem resolution outside the Woodlawn community; and (2) the institutional blockages and points of resistance which constitute an obstruction to community problem resolution.

This approach will not only provide the occasion for experimenting in an as yet uncharted area of goal-oriented modeling of social systems, but more importantly will build a major bridge between the Woodlawn Model Cities Plan and the city and metropolitan area.

Budget: This unit will aid the convenor in connection with his responsibility for all of the financing for the Core, whether derived from nonfederal public or private sources, federal non-Model Cities sources, or the federal Model Cities 80% funds constituting the Woodlawn share among the city's four Model Cities areas.

In this latter connection, the convenor and the budget unit will also receive and allocate the appropriate federal Model Cities funds to the two coordinate systems as well as among the Core: the HED and the WCB, thus assuring a pragmatic and administrative synthesis among all of the critical community activities.

Other Core Boards: In addition to the governing board, there will be created two special boards available for consultation to the convenor: an executive board of twenty elected by the governing board from among its members and a professional review board consisting of the operating heads of each of the functional subdivisions discussed below. Advisory councils of citizens will also be established in connection with each of the functional subdivisions.

Summary of Functional Divisions of the Core:[2] The Core will include four major functional divisions: health and social service, law, financial assistance, and environmental planning. The operating heads of the two coordinate systems—Education, Manpower and Housing and Economic Development—will be part of the convenor's Core consulting staff. The facilities associated with each of these functions constitute the backup to the outreach system discussed later.

Health and Social Service: This functional division has the following characteristics:

(1) The principal backup health facility proposed is a central Community Health Center to be owned, but not operated, by the community.

(2) Social Services are separated distinctly from the welfare financial support activities (the latter function being dealt with through an income maintenance program separately administered within the Core). Social Services will be located temporarily with the Community Health Center under the name, "The Community Service Clinic," and might in time be provided through the Social Service Center now under construction.

(3) Health and social service insurance programs proposed (with public and private funding) will be created either by the Core Corporation or by the proposed Housing and Economic Development Corporation. The insurance program would permit the medical and the social service patients and clients to purchase their services from the community-owned medical and social service facilities.

Financial Assistance: The income maintenance program, detailed later, will be the responsibility of this division and be separated from the social services currently associated with the welfare program.

Housing and Environmental Planning: This division will be responsible for housing, spatial planning, and land-use relationships, which will constitute a principal activity during later stages of the undertaking in which blueprints will be developed, reflecting social and economic proposals.

GOALS, OBJECTIVES AND STRATEGIES

Legal Services: Legal services will be made available via a Legal Aid Bureau and a method for engaging private legal advice. An important advocacy capability will thereby be provided to a population now generally shortchanged in this connection. Of equal significance, however, is the proposal that a Neighborhood Education and Conciliation Council be created.

General Comments: Although the Core encompasses a number of physical facilities, the question of proximity of these facilities is not central to our strategy. This is a decision which can be postponed pending the first-year pilot phase which is built into nearly all of the creative recommendations.

A hospital, nursing homes, and halfway houses (convalescent homes) are separately considered for independent creation and control, and, in any case, do not represent first-priority items, despite their importance.

The Core and Outreach System:
Outreach (the Pads)

Outreach facilities will be established throughout the community as the most effective means of dealing with the issue of delivery of services, a problem confronting every community and every profession nationally. These outreach facilities, Pads, while major in purpose and function, would be located in stores, basements, apartment complexes, houses, etc., and would multiply according to need. These Pads must take on a legitimate community-sanctioned complexion so as not to appear to be just another unrelated agency. The Pads would be manned by nonprofessionals—community agents selected from the area of service and then subjected to an intensive exposure and training by all of the related professionals. These community agents are generalists (although natural specializations may emerge), and they are expected to reach out to their community seeking contacts and opportunities to be of assistance in school-parent, doctor-patient, and other relationships. They will help solve problems, make referrals where necessary, call in professional functionaries as required, and, hopefully, deal with the preventive side as well as the crisis side. They will be equipped to perform many tasks which heretofore have been the exclusive provinces of the doctor, the social worker, the lawyer, the teacher, and other professionals. The Pads will include nurses on a regular basis, as needed, and will have regular visitations by the "back-up" professionals from the Core. The outreach facilities will cut across all functions included in the Core, will be open on a twenty-four hour basis, and will be independently constituted with an open committee of residents drawn from the Pads' area of service.

Just as the community convenor is the focus of the Core structure, so the Pad is the focus of the outreach operations; the real focus of both systems is the individual person or family living in Woodlawn. An individual enters the outreach system either as a single person entering the Pad or as a member of a small group such as a block club. Several block clubs, churches, and other social groups are to be organized into an open committee with which a paraprofessional works out of a local building called a Pad. In the Pad there will be a community leader, who is the person in charge, and a number of community workers (the staff), some equipment as specified in the various program com-

GOALS, OBJECTIVES AND STRATEGIES

ponents, technicians and visiting professionals. Most importantly, easy lines of access and communication will be available to the diverse institutions and back-up facilities located in the Core. A citizen who recognizes the community leader or community worker through social contact and who knows he is available to help with problems contacts him either in the street, in the Pad, or by phone and tells him the problem. If possible, the matter will be handled in the Pad by the services constantly or intermittently available there, but if this is not possible the community leader or community worker will go either himself or with the resident to the back-up offices in the Core that can handle the problem. The citizen leader or community worker will help the person as best he can, and it is his responsibility to know all about forms, practices, and regulations that the back-up facilities will require. At this point, the individual has passed into the Core operation. The outreach system is charted on page 84, but the particular technical assistance available in the Pad, as well as the training, is discussed next.

(1) The Pad will constitute a flexible device, shifting its location and the scale of its operations to reflect changes in Pad functions over time. Special skills will be incorporated as required to meet the needs, age cycles, and particular problems related to the population in the Pad's area of service.

(2) The Pad will maintain relationships outside of its physical location with the residents' homes, with the back-up facilities, and with the community at large in addition to the services performed in the Pad itself.

(3) The Pad will be oriented toward human service

needs, principally health, social service, education, employment, and law. Professionals will visit the Pad regularly and systematically to: (a) consult with Pad staff, (b) service clients and patients in those instances where more specialized service is required, and (c) assure the maintenance of standards for their particular professional performance.

(4) The Pad will have four primary functions: (a) community organization, (b) access to facilities, services, and institutions, (c) diagnosis, and (d) prevention and early treatment.

In the early stages of experience, the Pad will be expected to focus its attention on community organization, access, and diagnosis. With increased skill over time, prevention and early treatment will be emphasized and may become the central responsibility of the Pad.

(5) The citizen council (the open committee) for the Pad will recommend the person to be designated the Pad's community leader who, in turn, will recommend the community workers to the citizen council. The community leader (and, with the citizen council's approval, the community workers) will be selected from the Pad's area of service; the leader and workers will be people with sanctioned local ties, demonstrated capacities, and organizational skills. These recommendations will require concurrence by the Core convenor and the executive board of the Core's governing board.

The presumption is that the prime characteristics of the community leader and community workers are dedication, leadership capacity, recognition, and organizational potential. These individuals (the community leader and the community workers) will then need to undergo a period of training in the back-up facilities located in

GOALS, OBJECTIVES AND STRATEGIES

the Core so as to acquire and sharpen their skills in community organization, access, diagnosis, prevention, and early treatment. This training program will become an integral part of the program associated with the newly proposed Career Vocational Institute (discussed later).

The back-up facilities to which the Pad relates are associated with the three major systems proposed on a central basis for the community: the Core Corporation, the Housing and Economic Development Corporation, and the schools. Specifically, this includes the new legal devices proposed: the Community Health Clinic; the Community Service Clinic, which in time might be transferred and absorbed into the Social Service Center now under construction; the employment, business, and economic development activities; and the financial assistance section; among others.

This suggests that the community leaders and the community workers must be thoroughly familiar not only with the organizational arrangements thereby associated, but also with the professional requirements of each activity to a degree which enables them to perform professionally associated functions in the Pad related to each of the noted activities.

The input provided by the Pad staff in connection with diagnosis, prevention, and early treatment will constitute important material for the evaluation unit attached to the convenor.

WOODLAWN'S MODEL CITIES PLAN

CHART 2

The "Outreach" System

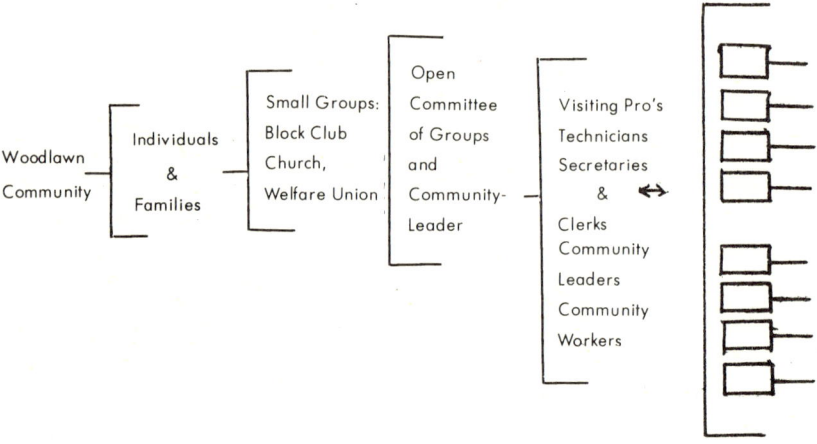

GOALS, OBJECTIVES AND STRATEGIES

The Education System[3]

The Woodlawn Community Board for Urban Education Projects (WCB) is the governing body of the current Experimental School District project and consists of twenty-one members with seven representatives each from the Chicago Board of Education, The Woodlawn Organization, and the University of Chicago. Action by the board requires a consensus of all three groups. This board, or some modification of it as experience may suggest, constitutes the community's principal school system policy board.

Six major activities will fall under the Woodlawn Community Board's aegis: (1) preschool centers, (2) primary schools, (3) middle schools, (4) Hyde Park High School, (5) a Cultural and Language Arts Center, and (6) fluid schools.

Ties to other activities will exist in various ways: to the outreach facilities in terms of parent contacts, home contacts, and via the fluid schools, augmented by parent participation in the schools and by parent councils; to the Housing and Economic Development Corporation, which will include the Career Vocational Institute, and via this instrument to all functions and activities connected with the training programs which will prepare all of the nonprofessionals to man the outreach facilities and the functional areas included in the Core; and to health, social service, and economic development in connection with the preschool centers, etc.

All funds allocated to Woodlawn by the city of Chicago, derived from the federal Model Cities sources (80%), will be reallocated by the Core Corporation; this includes all moneys for Woodlawn school purposes. In addition, the head of the Woodlawn Experimental Schools will serve as an added staff member on education to the convenor.

A planning and participation structure for the educational system, including special project advisory boards and parent councils relating to the Woodlawn Community Board, would incorporate the principle of "citizen responsibility" into all educational activities.

Housing and Economic Development Corporation (HED) [4]

A community development corporation provides an organizational mechanism to attract and exploit the capital and skills of the rest of the American society in a framework controlled from within the local community.

Three premises underlie the concept of the Housing and Economic Development Corporation: (1) it has a critical role to play along with government in the social betterment of a community; (2) community control is essential to the community if it is to develop a sense of pride and progress; and (3) government should assume a major responsibility in providing the seed money for the launching of a Housing and Economic Development Corporation.

In essence, HED is a nonprofit corporation operated by a group of paid professionals responsible to the community through a board of directors. The membership of the HED board should be composed of at least twenty-five community residents and businessmen.

This community public corporation will be created to undertake rehabilitation of existing housing, carry on new housing construction, shopping center development, and light industrial development.

GOALS, OBJECTIVES AND STRATEGIES

In addition, the corporation will seek to create insurance programs, particularly for health and social service, in order that patients and clients can buy their medical and social service care; establish credit institutions; generate spin-off development corporations; both own and stimulate business and residential development; and act as brokers for putting together development packages to be financed by others.

Except for greatly increased use of existing local devices (code enforcement and the like), and such instruments as the rent supplement program, turnkey, 221 (d) (3), cooperatives, and condominiums, no major public housing programs are contemplated. The principle reliance is on achieving improved housing via this Housing and Economic Development Corporation. There is included later a set of housing and environmental principles which will guide the provision of housing and the course of space-use in land development programs.

A major institutional activity which will be included in this corporation is a Career Vocational Institute, discussed later, with ties to the Experimental Schools (particularly the fluid schools), the Core, and the Pad.

Several avenues of funding for the HED are possible. To ensure community control, a certain amount would have to be raised within the community via a public stock subscription. Beyond this, funds could be raised from major insurance companies and foundations as well as local individuals and institutions—although stocks issued to non-community institutions would have to be non-voting shares.

Governmental funds might be obtained via a land grant (against which funds could be borrowed), bonds,
- leverage money from the Small Business Adminis-

tration (SBA), under the SBIC Act. In addition to the equity and working capital, other funds could be obtained from the SBA under Section 502 (similar to the money used for the Harper Court development in Hyde Park). The SBA will currently make loans of up to $100,000 and provide security for bank loans up to $350,000. It will arrange for special terms if ten or more businessmen can be brought together, as in the proposal for an industrial park or for a shopping center. The SBA plans to expand greatly its program of Economic Opportunity Loans (EOL) to black businessmen; these loans are for $25,000 at low interest rates (4.75%-5.50%) and are administered under the Chicago Small Business Opportunity Corporation (SBOC).

An effective means for organizing HED's work is the project management mode. This has the advantage of focusing all the resources on a sequence of projects and eliminates the categorization of activities into the old themes of housing, education, etc. Thus one section will concentrate on industrial development, another on black entrepreneurship, etc.

The HED will acquire expert knowledge of the entire economic life of the community in detail—its markets, resources, complementary industries, potential suppliers, facilities, and services—before business development is undertaken. To be effective, the HED should have a full-time staff to explore leads tenaciously, make contacts, handle promotions and correspondence, and keep on top of local development. They will also be responsible for raising community seed money generally required by lending institutions. Promising discussions are presently underway in these connections.

GOALS, OBJECTIVES AND STRATEGIES

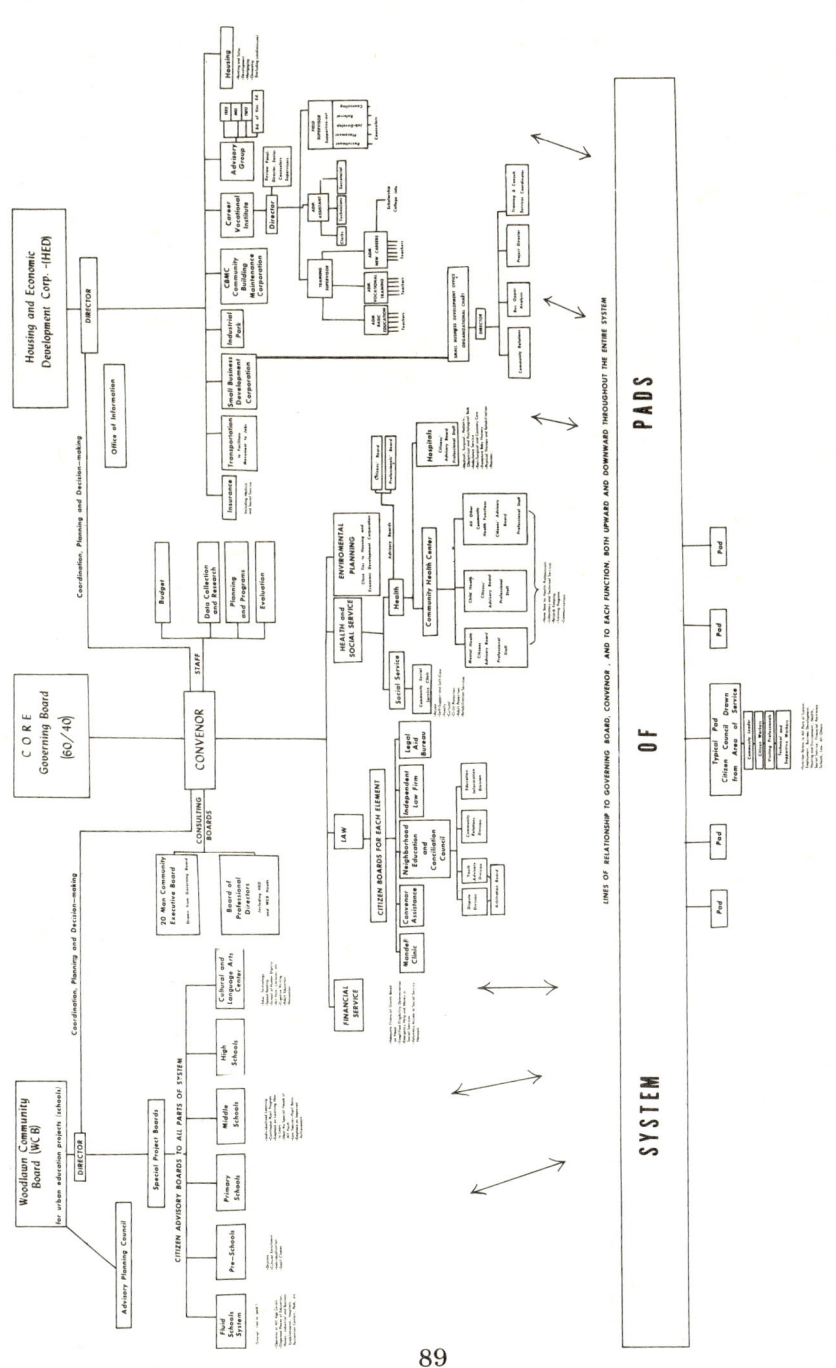

WOODLAWN'S MODEL CITIES PLAN

Footnotes

1. See copy of agreement between The Woodlawn Organization, the University of Chicago, and the Chicago Board of Education establishing the "Woodlawn Community Board for Urban Education" in the detailed Model Cities plan volume.

2. The Functional Divisions of the Core are elaborated in "Programmatic Components," p. 92.

3. The educational system is elaborated in "Programmatic Components," p. 138.

4. The HED is elaborated in "Programmatic Components," p. 151.

PROGRAMMATIC COMPONENTS

The network of proposed activities must be examined as an indivisible whole, subject only to minor qualification and modification. Disservice and damage will result by thinking of the constituent elements of this Model Cities "package" as negotiable commodities which established professions and service agencies can parcel out among themselves and upon which compromises can be reached. Rather, the dominant characteristic of the proposed system of program linkages is its reliance on "points of entry" for problem solving as opposed to the conventional professional absorption with a problem's "point of origin," a fixation which produces limited results.

Although the direct focus of our attention is the Woodlawn Model Cities target area, solving the problems of Woodlawn or any inner-city community depends in the long run on critical variables which are outside the target community. The debilitating effect of resistance by the surrounding society to the provisions of access to opportunities and to resources, and the barriers to upward mobility which face the inner-city population (even with demonstrated personal achievement) cannot be overestimated. Unless simultaneous changes of attitudes and institutions are effected in the cities and suburbs of America, Model Cities programs are likely to produce only temporary easing of ghetto suffering, followed ultimately by increased frustration and despair.

The proposals recommended here involve a series of adjustments by public and private institutions and agencies. An unwillingness or failure to make the modest accommodations necessary would raise serious question whether any appreciable value will come from the Model Cities instrument.

In addition, professional practice requires sharp modification. The proposals discussed later assume that programs associated with each of the professional fields can be brought into play selectively, and in various combinations, as part of a systematic problem-solving strategy. This strategy will replace the practice referred to earlier in which professionals participate only if permitted to expand their functions, administration, and bureaucracy.

Further, the proposals which follow introduce new strategic program linkages to replace the existing practice in which each agency expands its functions by accretion to include activities normally associated with other professional fields. Thus education's reliance on mental and physical health and on social service will be dealt with by integral programmatic accommodations and not by education developing a "health education" staff and programs, or health developing a "schools" staff and program, or social work developing an "educational staff;" and so on, ad infinitum. We find undesirable this current trend in which each functional system, while organized around a central activity, expands to include watered-down versions of all other related or allied functions.

THE CORE DIVISIONS

The fundamental Core Corporation, detailed above, consists of the following:

PROGRAMMATIC COMPONENTS

(1) A governing board of which (a) 40% of the members are elected at large and (b) 60% of the members are elected by community organizations on a delegate basis.

(2) A convenor (the executive), who receives local, state, and federal government funds, including Model Cities moneys, and private funds.

(3) Budget, programming, evaluation, and research staff functions.

(4) Functional components (discussed below): health and social services, environmental planning, financial service, and law.

(5) An outreach system (the Pads), manned by nonprofessionals located throughout the community, and performing many traditionally professional services.

HEALTH DIVISION OF THE CORE

The health component will have a board of directors composed of twenty-one community members and suitable executive staff of technical personnel to ensure sound day-to-day administration. Each member of this board of directors will have a three-year term of office, and seven will be elected from the community at large each year. The board of directors will be advised by an open-to-all community advisory board and an open-to-all professional advisory board. It will be empowered (via the Core) to receive local, state, and federal funds; to seek grants for training and research; to solicit foundations and other private donors; to receive funds from insurance companies and other third-party payers; and, generally, to be the responsible financial agent for the health services (see Chart 4).

For health, the board of directors will employ the senior administrative persons and staff necessary to administer, supervise, or operate a health delivery system. Health care will be financed by a combination of funds, but the basic system will be a capitation arrangement for comprehensive health services. Individuals in the Woodlawn community who can afford to support their own health care may do so by regular payments to an insurance underwriter responsible for collecting, appraising, and adjusting costs as necessary. The capitation fee will be established initially by experience with comparable systems throughout the country and then adjusted according to experience. The community might wish to assume these risks rather than assign them to an insurance underwriter.

For individuals who can afford only partial payment, populations currently defined as medically indigent but not at poverty levels, a sliding rate will be devised. This rate will be promptly responsive to improved or worsening personal financial conditions. This group is least provided for in current public financial support and yet its needs are pressing. Graded support from local and federal agencies is essential.

The financial support for populations defined as being at poverty levels of income will continue to derive from public sources but, rather than being provided in an episodic fashion per instance of illness, the public source would fund the corporation on a capitation basis for comprehensive health care, the amount to be established by the insurance carrier.

CHART 4

Health Organizational Arrangements

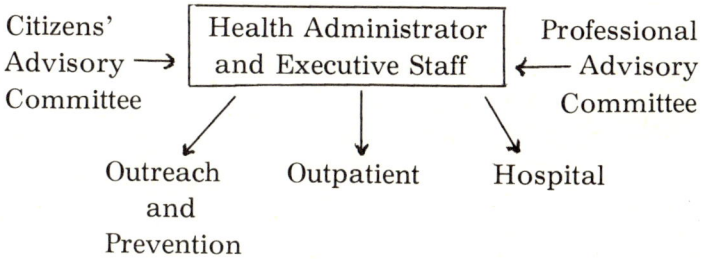

(The operating individuals and arrangements might vary such as individual and group practice, the Woodlawn Hospital, the University of Chicago, etc.)

Establishment of eligibility must be prompt, dignified, courteous, and with attention to maintaining the morale and self-esteem of the client. The determination should be made administratively and it should be disconnected from the actual delivery of service. At the site of delivery, each client should be treated equally; no one need know which client is funded through what source. Thereby one system of medical care will be established.

The board of directors, with the advice of the citizen and professional advisory boards and through its executive officers, will be responsible for negotiating contracts, agreements, and other arrangements with private practitioners, groups, agencies, hospitals, institutions, etc., to provide necessary service. Given administrative and financial control, they will be in a position to seek assessment of the quality of the services provided and to renegotiate the agreements as indicated.

This system provides opportunity for consumer and community participation in establishing priorities and in determining the type of system most valuable and useful. It also protects the professional in that it provides him ongoing freedom of choice about his participation and an opportunity for influencing decisions about the type of systems he considers to be optimal.

For individuals and professionals who prefer continuity of relationship between single patients, their families, and individual doctors, an opportunity should be provided for the establishment of capitation panels for individual practitioners and groups. In such an arrangement the individual or his family will obtain most of his medical and/or dental services from a particular professional; thereby the relationship as currently developed in fee-for-service models might be maintained.

The corporation might contract with agencies and institutions for certain services. For example, the Woodlawn Child Health and Woodlawn Mental Health Centers are already established systems delivering high-quality care not otherwise available.

The hospital component of the system will optimumly include resources at Woodlawn Hospital or another community hospital and back-up and special facilities at the University of Chicago Hospitals. Greater freedom of staff appointments and the opportunity for medical school relatedness, with the participation of medical students and house staff, would greatly enhance the professional attractiveness of these systems.

Informal discussions with insurance carriers suggest great interest in experimenting with the systems described. Although commitments were not requested and could not be made, we have the impression that explor-

PROGRAMMATIC COMPONENTS

ations about such systems could prove fruitful. Cost for such a capitation system under current arrangements and for this population might amount to approximately $200 per person per year, given East Woodlawn's current population of approximately 60,000 people, probably about equally divided among the indigent, medically indigent, and those able to pay. Cost estimates follow. Most observers believe that about 90% of the poverty group might eventually be enrolled; perhaps 60% of the medically indigent group; and perhaps 30% of those able to pay during a five-year period.

Such estimates would then provide the following participation and cost figures (see Chart 5).

CHART 5

Health Care Cost Estimates

	Total Population	Participating Population
Indigent	20,000	90% or 18,000
Medically Indigent	20,000	60% or 12,000
Self-supporting	20,000	30% or 6,000
Totals	60,000	36,000 @ $200/person =

Total yearly cost: $7.2 million

The portion of this cost which would be borne by public sources is approximately $4.8 million. The portion borne by individual responsibility would amount to

$2.4 million. Of course, as the income level within the community increased as a result of related programs, the public contribution would decrease.

Planning health services, like any other human service, must begin where people with health problems are. A mother with three children who has physical problems, whose first-grade child is having trouble adapting to school, who is behind in her rent, and who is receiving inadequate financial assistance cannot be expected to travel long distances for help. Nor can she be expected to approach in a sufficiently wise manner the several agencies from which she needs help. It is the burden of these agencies to provide nearby, comprehensive service centers that are inviting and welcoming in their atmosphere.

Health problems in East Woodlawn are interwoven with financial, legal, education, and many other human problems. To provide health services, then, in a sufficiently comprehensive way which takes into account the close link between health and all other human problems, a series of outreach facilities (the Pads) must be established. The outreach facilities (the Pads) will include the entire range of human services in addition to health. These facilities must provide diagnostic help of sufficient quality and quantity to tell accurately what the major human needs of any person in the area served by the center are. A community leader will be responsible for each such Pad and will direct a community service team of from five to eight community workers trained to make home visits, to collaborate with families in diagnosing the problems faced by a family member, and to carry out front-line help in the variety of human services involved in helping an individual overcome difficulties. In the health area, such a community worker

PROGRAMMATIC COMPONENTS

will interview a person in his home, gather a medical history, and even do certain basic diagnostic procedures such as taking a temperature, blood pressure, and other simple aspects of medical examination. In addition, the same community worker will be trained in interviewing techniques and sensitized to recognizing and understanding the emotional aspects of the person being interviewed. During such a home visit, the community worker could assess housing conditions and consult about legal matters while being available to go with the person with a problem to any of the second-line clinics in any particular professional area.

East Woodlawn requires approximately ten such Pads in the first year to take care of all needs. The community leader and the community workers form a team which includes workers who specialize in relating families to their local schools and in dealing with educational problems. All team members will be employed and paid by the community corporation. Recruitment for such team personnel will be carried out in the immediate geographic area served by the team.

The number of such facilities is based on the assumption that such facilities should be within a one to three-block radius of any individual in the community. From the mental health standpoint, the community workers will be able to do group therapy, to offer crisis counseling, to disburse medication prescribed by the psychiatrist, and do consulting for personnel based at the health center, as a back-up for all of the teams. Mental health professionals will be available for consultation to any team on request, and during special hours during the week these professionals would make rounds, visiting each of the teams and carrying out consultative, supervisory, and other functions.

Any individual suffering a more complicated health problem would be referred to the back-up health facility (the Community Health Center in the Core), where additional specialized professional help is available. However, the community worker involved in the referral would accompany the individual, making certain that the individual arrives at the clinic and receives the necessary care he or she requires. Followup treatment would be referred back to the Pad whenever possible.

Prevention is the primary goal of the Pad and will be carried out by two techniques. First, by not waiting for individuals to come to the Pad, the community service team will avoid falling into the traditional pitfall of the agency professional. The community team will have a primary mandate to make home visits to all individuals living in their geographic area, assess the status of families living in the area, and carry out remedial services where problems are found. From the practical standpoint, first priority will be given to strategically chosen age levels for help. For example, birth registration will automatically provide a stimulus for a home visit by a community worker.

Ambulatory Health Services

This proposal provides for complete ambulatory health services for all residents of the community. These services can be broadly categorized as:

(1) Preventive Health Services. These services include health education, immunization against disease, nutritional guidance, family planning, prenatal care and early detection of birth defects, metabolic disorders,

PROGRAMMATIC COMPONENTS

cardiopulmonary disease, mental illness and crippling dental disorders.

(2) Health Care for the Acutely Ill. Prompt attention is necessary for acute illness and emergency situations. Professional, laboratory, and X-ray services as well as the provision of medications and appliances are necessary.

(3) Health Care for the Chronically Ill. Comprehensive services should be provided to the chronically ill and the physically handicapped.

This health care system is organized to foster the earliest possible attention to health matters for all members of the community. Services should be provided for the entire family unit. Each family should be able to turn to a health care team and each physician, dentist, nurse, et al., should have the opportunity to care for members of a given family on a continuing basis.

The structure proposed for organization of ambulatory care may be divided into two major components. These are:

Outreach Facilities (PADS)

These posts, ten in number, will be located strategically throughout the community. They will be staffed by teams of public health nurses and community leaders with physicians serving as consultants, constituting the health component, but having functions related to all other professional areas since these Pads would be multipurpose facilities. They include the first line of health care.

Community Health Center

This facility will serve as the second line of health care service and will be located in the Core. It will provide (1) home base for health professionals; (2) location for major ancillary service including laboratory, X-ray, physical therapy, and pharmacy; (3) record-keeping center; and (4) base for personnel training programs.

While there may be advantages in providing several smaller health centers in the community, the advantages of reduced equipment and personnel needs favor a single center. Woodlawn is not a community that is difficult to traverse, and it would be possible to provide ambulance service to the center when necessary.

A decision regarding the optimum size of such a facility requires careful, detailed study. Based on data obtained from the U.S. Department of Health, Education and Welfare's document on planning outpatient facilities, however, it is estimated tentatively that 25,000 to 30,000 net square feet would be necessary.

It is recommended that flexibility guide the planners in their design. Such flexibility will encourage continuous appraisal and modification of the health system which is necessary if it is to grow optimumly to serve the community well.

The personnel needs of the center would be:

(1) Administrative. An administrative executive will manage personnel, patient flow records, and financial aspects of the center. The need for such an administrator is readily apparent when one considers the magnitude of such a complex and the increasing diversity of governmental and nongovernmental funding programs.

(2) Health Professionals. In this category will be in-

cluded physicians, dentists, nurses, medical social workers, pharmacists, and technicians. Many of these health professionals, as well as the allied nonprofessional health workers, will group into teams in order to provide adequately considered, total response to the patients' health needs. The number of physicians needed is dificult to accurately assess. The usual estimate is one physician per thousand, but it has also been estimated that the utilization of allied health workers to their fullest capacity may increase the physicians' efficiency by as much as 30%. It is hoped that this increased efficiency may be translated into a reduced number of required physicians. All common specialties—internal medicine, surgery, obstetrics, dentistry, pediatrics, psychiatry, opthalmology, orthopedics, urology, and otolarynogology—should be represented. The largest requirement will be for internists, pediatricians, and obstetricians; there will be less need for other specialty areas. Nursing personnel will be specially trained in as many instances as possible to increase their capabilities to do many tasks that are now done by the physician.

(3) Paramedical Personnel. Training programs for nonprofessional paramedical personnel will be built into the program. It is entirely possible to develop programs that will enable community people with nonmedical backgrounds to take on significant roles as physician's aides, dental assistants, medical technician assistants, file clerks, etc. Such programs will be well formulated and ongoing with opportunities and incentives for upward career mobility. Training will take place within the Career Vocational Institute (CVI) (see employment section). Likewise, it is possible to utilize persons with training as medical corpsmen, giving them the oppor-

tunity to use previously developed skills that might otherwise be wasted.

Facilities and services at the center include the following:

(1) Laboratory and X-ray facilities will be designed to provide all necessary data required for adequate outpatient care while avoiding, whenever possible, unnecessary duplication of facilities existing within available hospitals. The laboratory, for example, should be equipped to do routine hematologic studies, urinalysis, and common bacteriologic studies. It should be equipped with automated equipment wherever possible to increase its efficiency. The equipment should include an auto-analyzer so that routine blood chemical studies would be readily available. It should utilize microscopic techniques where possible, especially in determinations done on small children. Complex chemical and tissue studies should be referred to the hospital laboratory. The X-ray facility should allow routine radiologic evaluation, but no attempt at therapy should be made since this represents unnecessary duplication of elaborate equipment.

(2) A pharmacy will be included in order that patients may be provided medications under the umbrella of services extended by the center. The cost of medication is an important barrier to adequate health in the medically indigent populations. Provision of systems for the inclusion of medications is an important aspect.

(3) Day-care facilities which will be discussed later and will be located elsewhere are necessary so that well children may be properly attended while others in the family seek medical attention.

(4) A twenty-four hour holding facility would enable physicians to observe patients for a short time when

PROGRAMMATIC COMPONENTS

the need for hospitalization was in question. This reduces the number of unnecessary hospitalizations.

(5) Day and evening service should be provided and twenty-four hour emergency service is essential. Patients will be seen routinely by appointment but there will be adequate time in the appointment schedules to allow for care of the acutely ill. Personnel, time, and space must be provided for care of the emergency situation. Minor emergencies are treated in the facility and immediate care is provided for major emergencies.

(6) Record-keeping requires serious attention. Family records are more effective than individual records. This highly efficient mechanism provides more readily available insight into the understanding of illness as it affects a total family. Computerization of medical records should be accomplished to the greatest extent possible. Traffic planning for medical records should be adequate to readily locate records out of the central file. The system of record obtainment from the file should be rapid enough to provide immediate information on patients seen in the center as well as for patients visiting the outlying stations or confined to the hospital.

(7) A communications system that would place all personnel in easy contact with each other and with patients is vital to the success of such an operation.

(8) Adequate assessment programs will be built into the center's program in order to ensure that it was truly performing in the manner intended. Such assessment should include objective, nonbiased, designed studies preferably conducted by others than those providing the services. There should also be committees on medical practices and medical records to ensure high-quality performance.

It is important to consider how such a center would relate to both the outreach facilities and the hospital. We believe there should be constant interplay between all three. The readily available patient data should prevent unnecessary guesswork and expensive duplication of tests. More importantly, the interchange of personnel will provide an intimate working knowledge of the entire scheme. We believe that those physicians practicing at the center should staff the inpatient facility and should be directly involved in the care for their patients who are hospitalized.

Inpatient Services

Acute Hospital Facility

This facility will provide comprehensive hospital services for the participating population of Woodlawn so as to preserve the self-esteem of the individual. To this end, there will be no distinction among individuals based on their ability to pay. All participating members of the community will have prepaid comprehensive medical care insurance.

This program is designed also to ensure continuity of care to the community resident in his neighborhood while he is in the hospital and after his return to the community. As a means of ensuring this goal, we suggest that the community outreach component be involved in the advocate role. The community leader will know the individual or family from the beginning of illness to a return to health. The "advocate" of the hospitalized individual will become a temporary integral part of that individual's health team and will seek to provide such

PROGRAMMATIC COMPONENTS

detailed information regarding the patient's home and family situation as to allow the team to make more rational assessments and to conceive more realistic plans for use both in the hospital and out.

There are insufficient acute inpatient facilities in all categories of medical care on the south side of Chicago. Several outmoded facilities should be replaced within five years. At least 500 new beds must be constructed before the area can meet its own needs without exporting patients to distant sites. A new 400-500 bed hospital should be located in or near the Woodlawn area to serve primarily that area and other nearby areas in the general study area (potentially, community areas 39, 41, 42, 43, and 69). If this hospital could be organized on the base of existing professional personnel and institutions, it would facilitate its establishment and reduce its cost. However, such an institution must be responsive to community need. This provision can be accomplished only by citizen participation from the East Woodlawn area and other nearby communities represented on its board of directors. This hospital board of directors is not identical with the Core community corporation. Rather, each will be independent of the other, and inpatient health care will be arranged on a contract basis. It must have an open medical staff. Care must be taken to synthesize this institution into a total health system. The major medical specialties should be represented by facilities which reflect the age distribution and disease prevalence rates in the Woodlawn community.

The structure of the acute hospital should include a variety of different types of nursing units: (1) medical, surgical, pediatric, obstetrical, and psychiatric beds; (2) an ambulance and transportation service which would carry patient, family, health staff, community leader, and medical supplies from the outreach site to the hospital and patient's home; (3) special care units such as post-surgical and coronary units; (4) a premature nursery; (5) a physical therapy and rehabilitation unit; and (6) a pharmacy coordinated with outpatient pharmacy functions.

There should be intensive care and coronary surveillance units ranging from those providing for the most intense medical and nursing supervision through "ordinary care units" to ambulatory care units which allow the patient to carry on as much of a normal adult life as his disabilities permit.

Psychiatric services should be provided in a comprehensive community mental health center which would serve not only Woodlawn but other communities as well. A five-year goal is a community mental health center for this area providing comprehensive psychiatric services, funded through federal Community Mental Health Center construction and staff grants, and the State of Illinois Department of Mental Health.

Extended Care Facilities

Following discharge from the acute general hospital there may still be need for medical care beyond the capabilities found in the home. This need will be met by extended care facilities in the community. In all instances these facilities will be served by the same medical staff and the *same community leader* (advocate) as in the acute general hospital and outreach facility. It is expected, however, that the ratio of physician to non-physician staff will be lower in the extended care facilities than in the acute general hospital. There will be additional job opportunities for community residents in these facilities. In these extended care facilities the link of the patient to his home and community will continue through the community leader who will be continually involved with the patient while in this facility and will keep him in contact with his family and his friends. These facilities include:

(1) A nursing home to provide care for geriatric patients and have a gradation of units from a homelike setting with very little supervision by the health staff to more elaborately equipped and fully staffed units for the bedridden. These older individuals could serve as a salaried and volunteer community resource to *be called by the community leaders* for various roles. These jobs or activities might include (a) foster grandparents, (b) temporary homemakers, (c) workers in child day-care centers, etc.

(2) A halfway house to serve those psychiatric patients who do not need hospitalization but who cannot yet function in the home.

The medical staff will service the above health facilities. In addition, to attract highly competent medical persons and to maintain their level of competence, there should be a teaching affiliation with the University of Chicago with a well-defined system for consultation and referrals for unusual cases. Such arrangements alleviate the necessity for duplicating in the Woodlawn Community Hospital expensive, rarely used, but necessary diagnostic and treatment facilities. Residents of Woodlawn in need of such facilities would be readily accepted at the University of Chicago services already in operation.

Training Within the Health Facilities

The health facilities will provide many and varied training opportunities for the residents of the community. It is a prime aim of this health facility to enhance the skills and earning power of community residents. To this end, the staff of the health facilities will be charged with developing, in connection with the Career Vocational Institute, training programs in, for example, the following areas: (1) medical and laboratory technicians, (2) nursing service personnel, (3) clerical and secretarial personnel, (4) business and administrative personnel, (5) maintenance personnel, and (6) dietary personnel.

Importantly, the health facility will also furnish training and certain health skills to the community leaders. Whenever possible community residents will take the lead in the training of their fellows. Jobs for persons trained by such programs will be readily available in institutions outside the community, and within Woodlawn employment will be likely available in Pads, community-developed small businesses, and other Woodlawn-related projects.

Immediate and Long Range Aims

The large amount of planning, the financial investment, and the time for construction necessary to build the acute hospital will delay its availability. The outreach and outpatient facilities will be established before any type of integrated inpatient service. The hospital, then, is a five-year goal rather than an immediate possibility. This time lag provides the opportunity to

PROGRAMMATIC COMPONENTS

train and develop the community leaders and to try out various aspects of the programs described in this and other sections. In the first years, full utilization should be made of existing hospital facilities in and around the Woodlawn community. While no single hospital could absorb the patient load of the Woodlawn community, it is hoped that the combination of these hospitals will provide adequate temporary medical coverage while the planning and construction of a general hospital in the Woodlawn community is under way.

Physicians who staff the outreach and outpatient facilities should have hospital privileges at the hospitals in the vicinity of Woodlawn. Continuity of care from the community into the hospital and back again would thereby be ensured.

Physicians already in practice in and around Woodlawn will be encouraged strongly to participate in the total health care delivery system. Staff members of the hospital mentioned who do not presently practice in the immediate environs will likewise be encouraged to participate.

SOCIAL SERVICES DIVISION OF THE CORE

The Social Welfare Committee has used a number of approaches in developing a proposal to alleviate many of the gaps and inequities in social service available to Woodlawn residents. Demographic data and interviews with agency personnel and with a large number of community residents have provided the background of community needs.

The federal guidelines for social services (from the

Social Security Act as amended) and discussions with members of the social work and other helping professions have provided a basic framework for this segment of the planning.

We recommend the complete separation of financial service and social service. Social services should be available to anyone in the community who requests them regardless of his financial status. Financial service should be available to those who need it without obligation to accept social service. Social Service in time should be part of a combined health and social service insurance program to enable the consumer to purchase care and service and provide him or her with choices. This could be achieved by expanding the health insurance program discussed earlier.

The combination of social service and financial service has been too long used to excuse the respective deficiencies of each.

Most welfare workers do not have the time to treat their clients as individuals and actually carry out a plan for service. Problems and tasks relating to financial service have the highest priority. In addition, few workers have the specialized training necessary to provide social services which can go beyond the minimal requirements of eligibility determination and redetermination. To many clients the worker's prime function is seen as that of policeman or investigator, and the clients rarely see the social worker as a person to help with anything not directly related to financial service.

There is a serious question about the welfare department's ability to provide effective social service when it also must be responsible for determining financial eligibility and the amount of a client's assistance. Welfare

PROGRAMMATIC COMPONENTS

regulations and service needs are often in conflict. Regulations regarding referral for employment, establishment of paternity, and "the man in the home" among others make it difficult for worker and the client to establish a relationship based on mutual trust and respect.

Organizational Framework for Social Services

Social services will be provided within the Core in a combined Health and Social Service Division, and as part of the outreach facility (the Pad).

Within this division in the Core, a Social Service Clinic will be established and staffed by professional social service personnel, as well as by nonprofessionals, and governed by a board of Woodlawn citizens to whom the director of the Social Service Clinic will be responsible. This Social Service Clinic will constitute the back-up facility to the Pad and have the closest relationship to the health component. In time, the Social Service Center now under construction under the auspices of the University of Chicago School of Social Service Administration and funded by the federal government may assume this back-up facility role.

The community leaders and community workers in the Pad will assume front-line responsibility for the delivery of social services, have access to the social service back-up facilities, and have consultations and other contacts with appropriate professionals as is the case with all other professional services.

The Social Service Clinic should be located as close to the financial service office (discussed later) as possible for the convenience of persons using both. Staff will include professionally trained workers serving primarily as supervisors and consultants for social services, agency trained social workers (college graduates without professional social work training), community resident workers, and volunteers. Social service staffs could be assigned according to the worker's competence rather than by the usual arithmetic assignment of cases. Community resident workers would play a vital role in providing social services and would be helped to develop skills through training, seminars, and workshops. Community workers in the Pad will be trained to provide social services and to refer anyone who needs social or financial services beyond the skills of the Pad workers.

The community leaders and workers would help the professional social work staff in the central facility understand the community and become more attuned to the problems and needs of Woodlawn residents. The Social Service Clinic and the Pad staff would provide group and community services such as programs on budgeting, homemaking, child care, and community planning, as well as the more traditional social services.

Access Services

One of the most crucial of all services is that of access: assistance in establishing eligibility, crisis intervention, interpretation and referral, advocacy and outreach. In a community where existing services are fragmented and those in need of service are often unsophisticated, aggressive and comprehensive outreach services are a must, and this will be one of the four major functions of the Pad.

Many of the services referred to in the material that follows are provided by other program components in connection with employment, legal services, etc., but concern for the provision of social services remains a function of the Social Service Clinic.

Self-Support Services

Self-support services include counseling, evaluation of potential for self-support, vocational training, placement, and day care. A particularly essential service area for encouraging self-support is that of adolescent opportunity: job training, counseling, and placement for teenagers.

In self-support services there are two critical unmet needs at the present time: more and better job training programs, especially for welfare recipients, and more day-care centers. There can be no hope of increasing the number of self-supporting persons in Woodlawn until these two priorities are met.

*Services to Mothers and
Their Children*

Services to mothers and their children involve five general areas: prenatal and postnatal medical care, assistance during the period of confinement, personal counseling, birth control information, assistance in seeking legal services for the establishment of paternity and child support, and environmental services to help the mother and child make suitable living arrangements.

The counseling and environmental services are the most urgently needed services for mothers and their children. Birth control information must be more publicly dispersed. Finally, the legal services for support in establishing a paternity must be more readily available to public assistance clients who wish to use them.

WOODLAWN'S MODEL CITIES PLAN

Services to Strengthen Family Life

Services to strengthen family life are directed toward enhancing child development, preventing desertion, achieving reconciliation, maintaining ties between parents and children in broken marriages, and providing legal assistance when necessary.

Cultural Services

It is not enough to have adequate housing, income maintenance programs, and sufficient health services. These are prerequisites for a thriving community but are not ends in themselves. When these basic needs are satisfied, the community will be able to make use of those services which contribute to the enrichment of life.

There is a serious lack of cultural services in Woodlawn. There is a branch of the Chicago Public Library, and various social and recreational groups organize field trips and day camp activities, but these are not adequate for a community of Woodlawn's size. The nature of the cultural services must be determined by the community and such services must be staffed by community residents.

Protective Services for Children

Children who are neglected or abused must have adequate protective services; the community must also be aware of these services. Services include counseling with the parents, foster care of the children when children must be removed from the home, legal services when custody of the children is involved, and services to

PROGRAMMATIC COMPONENTS

help parents provide an adequate home for their children.

Protective services for children should also include special education or training for children whose physical, mental, or emotional impairments make it difficult or impossible for them to benefit from regular schooling.

In addition, the community should have a halfway house for children. The house would accommodate children who are without parents or guardians awaiting placement in foster homes, and children who are released from custodial institutions, such as the Audy Home. The building should not give the appearance of a reformatory, but should allow a healthy atmosphere and access to the community for children.

Adult Protective Services

Protective services are also necessary for adults who, because of physical or mental impairments, are unable to manage their affairs without assistance. Necessary services include securing guardianship or other legal assistance, helping the individual to obtain safe, comfortable living quarters, assisting him to obtain housekeeping services or home-delivered meals so he may remain in his own home. Other services include counseling and involvement in social and community activities.

*Rehabilitation Services for Blind
and Disabled Adults*

An effective rehabilitation service includes counseling and evaluation, physical restoration services (including corrective medical treatment and prosthetic appliances), vocational training, and child placement. The handicapped must have also an organization or group to assume the role of advocate to ensure that prospective candidates are accepted for training and that employers understand that a handicapped person can be a productive employee.

FINANCIAL SERVICES DIVISION OF THE CORE

The function of a financial service system is to maintain income. The following is a proposal for a financial service system, administered by a division within the proposed Core Corporation, designed to achieve this goal. The key differences between this proposed system and the current system are independence from the social service system, adequacy of assistance levels, and reorganization of eligibility determination. The discussion which follows refers to each component of the system, describing its function and comparing it briefly with the present aid system.

Who is Eligible

All neighborhood residents who meet the single criterion of financial need will be eligible for the available services under the proposed plan. This will require a number of revisions in current practices. The current categories of aid recipients would be eliminated, with all needy people treated equally. Even families with one or more members employed will be eligible if their level of earnings falls below prescribed standards. Present legal definitions of "dependents" for eligibility determination would remain unchanged. (See detailed Model Cities plan volume for "Draft of Proposed Eligibility Declaration.")

PROGRAMMATIC COMPONENTS

Reception and Application

The financial service office will be run as a business-like public service enterprise, as a separate division within the Core, using local residents as much as possible to take and process applications and to make adjustments.

Upon entrance to the financial service office, attention to the client's request for assistance will be available immediately. Reception personnel will be local residents, adequately trained to administer the application process and supported by professional supervisors and community volunteers where applicable. Welfare rights, policies, and procedures will be carefully and courteously explained to all applicants and newly designed literature reiterating this information will be given to them. If required, the reception and application processing staff will provide the illiterate applicant with assistance.

The actual aid application procedure will involve the barest minimum of paperwork. Also, each applicant will be given the option of executing the required paperwork at home.

Eligibility Determination

Upon completion of the required orientation and the application process, the applicant will be required to sign an affidavit of need, to confirm his legal eligibility for financial services. The affidavit has been designed to meet all the various state and federal legal requirements for financial aid eligibility.

The affidavit will substitute for the currently exhaustive, and often insulting, investigation of applicant eligibility. The affidavit procedure will be executed by the intake clerk.

In cases where one of the child's parents is not in the home, applicants will be asked only whether child support proceedings have been instituted; if none has been, applicants will be required to sign a pledge to the effect that such action would be taken. The client will be also offered information regarding legal services available in the community.

A small percentage sample of applications and affidavits will be reviewed routinely for accuracy and legal proceedings will be initiated in the event of detected fraud.

Eligibility will be redetermined periodically by written communications from the financial service office to the client. A simple form will indicate changes in the client's financial situation which might affect his eligibility or grant level. Return of the redetermination forms will be required to continue public assistance payments for the succeeding period. This simple mail procedure will eliminate the quarterly home visits currently required by caseworkers in order that eligibility be re-established. Redetermined eligibility cases also will be subject to sampling and detailed review for accuracy.

The Financial Grant

The financial grants to be received by clients in Woodlawn will be increased significantly from present aid levels. The objective of the proposed aid program is to ensure every neighborhood resident a minimum income equal to a level sufficient to meet reasonable family needs. Chart 6 depicts graphically how the proposed grant system will work and how it will differ from the present aid scheme.

PROGRAMMATIC COMPONENTS

Every Woodlawn family eligible for financial service will be entitled to a level of family income equal to an agreed upon standard for a family of that size.

For example, in Illinois, a family of four with no income currently receives only $2,544 per year in public assistance grants exclusive of special allowances.

Under the proposed plan, the same family will receive a basic grant of $4,078, an amount determined by the community Social Welfare Committee to be an adequate minimum. This proposed amount is also very close to the grant level which several government studies show to be a realistic minimum grant to support a family of four living in an urban area in Illinois. The grant level will be reduced by $500 for each number below four or increased by $400 for every additional family member.

By raising grants to ensure all recipients an acceptable level of income, it will be unnecessary to request budget changes or special grants each time special school supplies, furniture, or clothing were needed.

The grant will be a flat amount, sufficient in size to cover the client's needs, and the present system of supplementary grants will be eliminated.

Responsibility for budget management will be placed in the hands of the client, who will have complete discretion over how he budgets and spends the grant. If budgeting assistance were desired, however, the financial service office will provide this help to the client.

Those who are able to work will be entitled to a work premium so that families which earned some income could enjoy total financial resources in excess of the standard support level. The size of the work premium for families earning some of their own income will vary on a sliding scale according to the amount earned. Once earned income plus work premium reached $5,250 for a family of four, no additional work premiums would be paid for increased work. (See Chart 6.)

The work premium is proposed only as a means of helping a family get to an earning level where it can be self-supporting.

Families which are earning above the basic support level and have not been on public assistance will not be eligible for work premium benefits.

Once the earned income of a family which has been on assistance rises above the basic level, the family would cease to be eligible for continued assistance over the long term.

The Emergency Service Unit

Any financial applicants in need of immediate consultative services or personal assistance will be referred at the time of application to the emergency service unit, which will be staffed by professional social workers and paraprofessional assistants.

Referral to the emergency service unit will be voluntary on the part of the applicant.

The emergency service unit will be equipped only to provide social services immediately needed by the client. Longer term needs will be met by community social services.

The emergency service unit will have at its discretion also a small pool of cash funds which it can disperse to clients facing financial emergencies.

Clients will be free to accept or reject referral to the social service network without danger of jeopardizing their financial assistance eligibility or grant level.

Referrals to the Social Service Network

At the time of financial assistance application, the client will be given information explaining community social services and the service facilities available to all Woodlawn residents.

The applicant will be advised to study the community service literature to determine whether he might be interested in utilizing any of the services.

At the request of the applicant, the intake worker could refer the applicant directly to the social service network.

It may be possible for the Welfare Union to serve in a liaison function. The Welfare Union could provide an invaluable service in helping clients adjust to their new circumstances and in advising them on matters pertaining to social services. In providing such service, funds to subsidize the Welfare Union would be provided.

Clerical and Accounting

Clerical and accounting functions will be greatly simplified over current aid systems because the need for extensive case work files and supplemental grants will be eliminated.

To permit a period of experimentation with this new financial service program, and to enhance the possibility of securing a special pilot grant from the Department of Health, Education and Welfare, it will be necessary to *fix* the universe of welfare recipients for an initial period to test the proposal. Consequently, to establish the universe, for two years from the time of initial undertaking, welfare recipients will need to have resided in the East Woodlawn area for six months prior to the test assistance program launching to be eligible for entry into the new program. Residents who did not meet this residence requirement would still, of course, be eligible for current welfare grants.

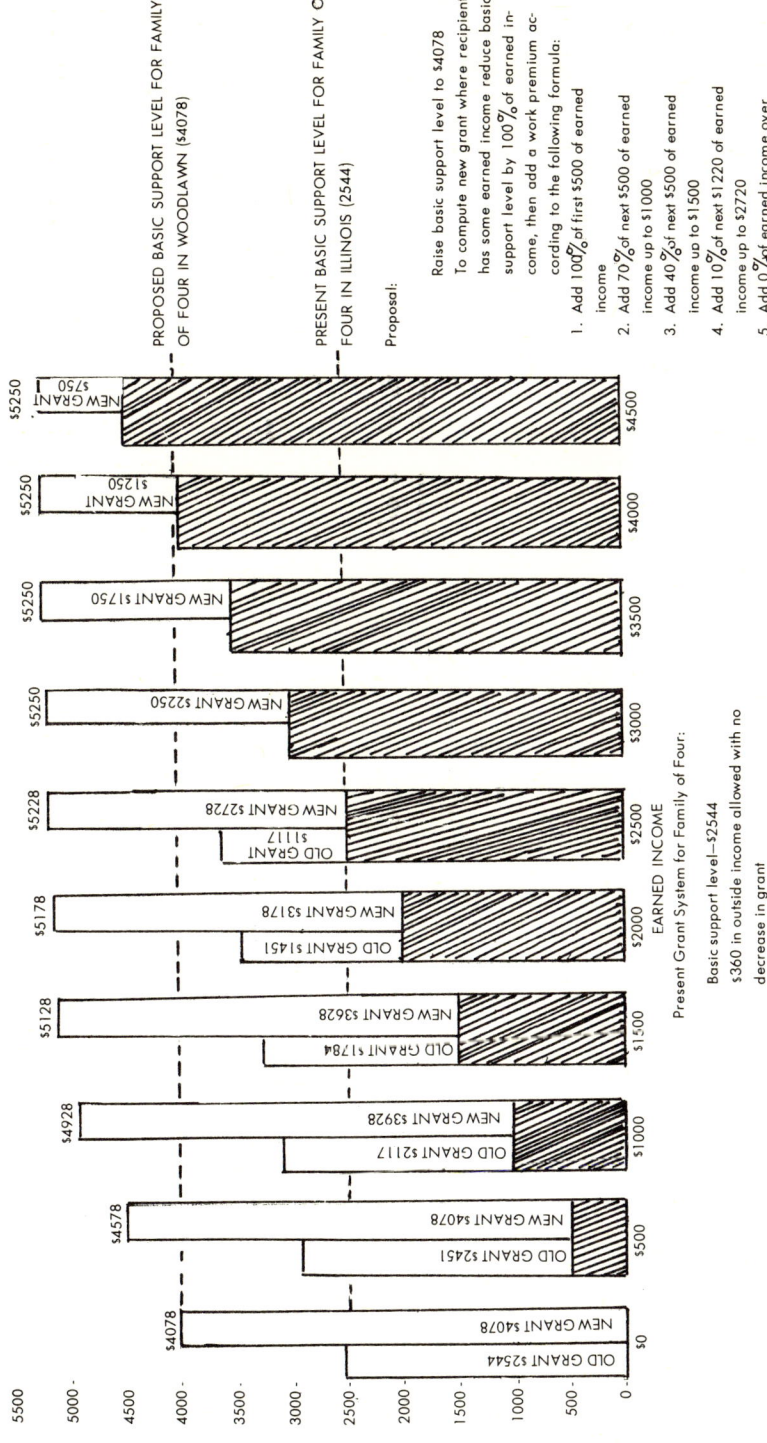

CHART 6. THE FINANCIAL GRANT SYSTEM

LAW DIVISION OF THE CORE

The Woodlawn Legal Service Program, a part of the Law Division within the Core Corporation, attempts to establish a comprehensive structure under which the community and the legal system will interact so as to facilitate proper functioning of the law for everyone.

An Outline of the Woodlawn Services Program

The Individual Components

Social Service Clinic[1] *and Financial Assistance Division within the Core—Legal Service Component: The Legal Aid Bureau (LAB).* This component will perform most or all of the remedial case work for "eligible" clients which is presently performed by the legal aid clinics in the University of Chicago Law School and the Woodlawn Urban Progress Center.

Independent Neighborhood Law Firm. This component will fill the gaps left by the traditional legal aid approach and perform a variety of new forms of legal services, retaining the flexibility necessary to develop better relations with private attorneys and to try new legal theories.

Neighborhood Education and Conciliation Council (NECC). This component will perform a variety of functions. In general, it will settle intraneighborhood disputes by discussion or arbitration, disseminate information to all citizens concerning their rights and responsibilities within the legal system, and attempt to assist in the creation of a better police-community relationship.

PROGRAMMATIC COMPONENTS

The Convenor. The Core corporation will be assisted by providing it with four attorneys as house counsel.

The University of Chicago: Mandel Clinic. This component, staffed by Law School faculty and students, will perform a variety of functions. In general, it will assist in the preparation and presentation of trial, test, and appellate cases which originated in the Social Service Clinic intake, draft relevant legislation, prepare treatises with legal problems of community concern, and conduct preliminary training for "community lay advocates." In addition to its interdependent relationship with the Social Service Clinic, this component will cooperate closely with all community agencies.

The Structure of the Woodlawn Legal Services Program

Each of the five components will function as an individual unit, and each will be responsible to the director of the Woodlawn Legal Services Program all as part of the Law Division within the Core. The director will be chosen by and be responsible to the board of directors of the Law Division and its executive committee.

The Individual Components in Detail

The Social Service Division of the Core—Legal Service Component:—

The Legal Aid Bureau

The Legal Aid Bureau will be initially composed of seven attorneys (selected by the Legal Aid Bureau in consultation with the board of directors), three secretaries and eight assistants (chosen by the NECC in conjunction with the seven attorneys). In order to meet the anticipated increase in requests for legal services, the staff will expand to twelve attorneys, seven secretaries, and twelve legal assistants, within one or two years of commencement.

A major function will relate to any acquisition of property by the Department of Urban Renewal and other public agencies. This bureau will make the services of appraisers and legal counsel available to the property owner to ensure a fair price for the sale of property, as well as to tenants, to provide protection in connection with relocation and other tenants' rights.

Several changes are envisioned which will improve the services now performed by the two existing legal aid offices. The Bureau will cooperate with the Public Defender's office in obtaining better representation in cases that the Legal Aid services are unable to accept, by means of a comprehensive "case information form" which will facilitate the Public Defender's representation. The form will include space for comment or suggestion by the interviewing attorney concerning points of law on which a defense might be based.

Another aspect of the criminal legal services will be the development of new procedures for handling juvenile offenders. Coordination with the Youth Advisory Section of the NECC, the Joint Youth Development Commission (JYDC), and the Juvenile Courts will be part of the new procedure. Legal Aid attorneys will be charged with the responsibility of demonstrating to the Juvenile Court the value of the recommendations of the Youth Advisory Section and the JYDC.

PROGRAMMATIC COMPONENTS

Existing legal services for family problems could be greatly improved and expanded. The Legal Aid Bureau will be strengthened by staffing the legal component of the Social Service Clinic of the Core with the following: (1) two legal assistants to interview and prepare cases and (2) one attorney to handle the court work. The volume of cases will be reduced by provision of a reconciliation service in the Social Service Clinic.

A significant proportion of the present Legal Aid caseload is concerned with questions of welfare law. The Bureau will employ two legal assistants who are knowledgeable and experienced in the mechanics of welfare agency regulations.

Finally, to facilitate accessibility of the Bureau to more residents, volunteer, indigenous lawyers will visit Pads during certain evening hours. NECC will inform the community of the availability of these attorneys.

The Independent Neighborhood Law Firm

The firm will be composed of five attorneys chosen by the director of the Woodlawn Legal Services Program, three secretaries chosen by the attorneys, and four legal assistants chosen by the NECC in consultation with the attorneys.

The firm will provide legal services on a more flexible scale of eligibility than present LAB or OEO standards permit. The firm will handle cases of marginal eligibility on a partial fee basis. A sliding scale of eligibility or an individual decision as to what a client can afford in relation to the case presented will be utilized. The remaining part of the standard fee will be paid by funding agencies directly to the firm.

The practice of the firm will be far reaching in that it will be involved in community matters through class actions or taxpayers' suits; it will be able to hire non-legal professionals to assist where appropriate; and it will invite local attorneys to participate in its activities as either paid consultants or on a contractural basis. It will make its services available to the community leaders and community workers in the Pads as individual needy clients and families are identified.

The Neighborhood Education and Conciliation Council (NECC)

This component and the neighborhood firm represent the major areas of innovation in the Legal Services program. The NECC is designed to handle intracommunity, economic, and social problems with legal implications.

Because of the diverse nature of the service it will perform, the NECC will have its own internal structure. Primarily responsible for its activities will be the director of the NECC.

The NECC will be divided into five divisions, each having a separate function:

The Dispute Division. This division will be composed of one local attorney, chosen by the NECC Director, as a part-time salaried supervisor; one *Vista* attorney, chosen by the NECC Director as a full-time supervisor; three salaried lay advocates, chosen by the NECC Director; and four VISTA volunteers, or fact-finders.

The Dispute Division will handle all totally intracommunity disputes (with the exception of juvenile, criminal, and family service matters), either by direct initial contact with the client, or by referral from another legal service component or from a Pad.

Youth Advisory Division. This division will handle matters involving youths. Heretofore, the Joint Youth Development Commission has played a role in these matters, and this report assumes that a pattern of cooperation can be established with JYDC. The activities of this division will revolve around the settlement of disputes involving juveniles, as well as the encouragement of parental responsibility for juveniles who might otherwise be processed through the Juvenile Court system. The cooperation of the Police Department will be essential; in addition, the Youth Advisory Division will offer the police its services.

The Youth Advisory Division will be set up in the same manner as the Dispute Division, except that here the fact-finders will be local youths, rather than VISTA's.

Arbitration Board. In the event that the Dispute Division or Youth Advisory Division has failed to achieve an acceptable conciliation between the adverse parties, the dispute will be sent to the Arbitration Board, with the parties' consent. This component will be composed of one local youth, one Core staff member, one local social service member, and one local attorney—all unsalaried volunteers who will meet once weekly.

Information and Education Division. This division will be composed of one legal assistant chosen by the director of the NECC and one VISTA volunteer. The division will disseminate materials and plan community meetings to inform Woodlawn citizens of their rights and liabilities under the law, and how to act on the basis of these through the Woodlawn Legal Services Division.

Community Relations Division. The director of the NECC will select one local citizen to direct this program. Together with the NECC Executive Committee and Director, he will begin a program of police relations in the Woodlawn community. This will include not only opening the channels of communication between the police and the community by means of joint meetings and publication of mutually educational materials, but also provisions for the election of a Civilian Review Board to meet with the Grand Crossing police to review and discuss specific reported instances of objectionable police and civilian behavior. Where juvenile matters are presented, this division will work closely with the Youth Advisory Division.

Community Organizations

The attorneys who will act as counsel to the community organizations will be VISTA attorneys. (At present there are four VISTA attorneys working with T.W.O. as part of the Community Legal Counsel Program.)

THE UNIVERSITY OF CHICAGO: MANDEL CLINIC

This component will be composed of one University professor and one University Bigelow Teaching Fellow, three secretaries, and members of the Mandel Clinic

Legal Aid Association chosen by the two staff men. As noted above, this component will cooperate closely with all other components of the Woodlawn Legal Services Program as well as perform its own functions.

ENVIRONMENTAL PLANNING DIVISION OF THE CORE

Environmental planning and development in Woodlawn will not rely on land clearance as the principal means for achieving community housing goals but will operate according to the planning principles recited below. The means for realizing these principles in practice will be a public community corporation for both housing and economic development. However, the environmental planning itself will be undertaken as a division within the Core. Hopefully, what would be achieved is a pool of funds to implement the environmental planning proposals to aid existing owners in the improvement of their property, facilitate new construction, and encourage new forms of ownership and entrepreneurship.

The principles governing the operations of this corporation follow:

(1) Planning is required for both Woodlawn and in connection with changes in, and effect on, surrounding areas, particularly to the west and southeast, as well as in connection with issues requiring a city and metropolitan area perspective. Put positively, as the Woodlawn community restores itself, simultaneous improvement in physical circumstances and in individual and family opportunities must be dealt with on a much larger geographic basis.

(2) Housing involves much more than simple shelter

since living accommodations are an important part of the larger physical and social context of the Woodlawn community. Therefore, planning for housing will be part of overall planning of the physical environment, which will be expressive of the social processes and needs of this residential community.

(3) In connection with the environmental emphasis discussed immediately above, it is essential to view the changes in the environment as the means by which other important goals are reciprocally achieved, i.e., the enhancement of job-generating opportunities, school and health facilities, etc. Therefore, any measures that are proposed to deal with physical change in Woodlawn should be supported by evidence that the changes recommended serve the social and economic needs of the people within Woodlawn and are not being undertaken for purely esthetic reasons, or because they are required or desired by special-interest professionals, solely for purposes of efficiency, or to facilitate citywide administration.

(4) The residents of the Woodlawn community should be relied on to determine the physical character of the community which they would like to see created by the planning process, in order to assure that the environment reinforces the style of life reflecting the desires of the residents themselves. For example, the community could determine the character of land uses which the community wishes to encourage, i.e., housing, shopping, industrial development, institutional growth and public facilities, including schools, parks, etc.

(5) No detailed lot-by-lot or block-by-block physical plan is sought. Rather, what is sought is a plan which would set in motion a process of continuous planning for change as well as the plan's undertaking to reflect

PROGRAMMATIC COMPONENTS

the changing needs of Woodlawn residents; the expanding opportunities which will hopefully emerge over time; and the aids, both public and private, which are developed at various points in the future. This process can best be achieved by a plan which combines a limited number of physical recommendations together with a series of policy recommendations as follows:

(a) The physical plan will include those fixed elements which will provide a basic frame of development for the Woodlawn community, i.e., the basic traffic and circulation of the community; the identification of open spaces, school sites and other critical public spaces; the identification of institutional spaces; and, most important, those community focal points around which the service needs of the community will be met. These latter focal points will simultaneously provide Woodlawn with a physical translation of its social aims and purposes.

(b) Along with this general physical frame, a series of policy statements will be developed which will guide the individual actions of the private and public sector, i.e., policies with respect to housing types, the character of institutional and industrial development, the character of ownership including the attitude toward public housing, rent supplements, etc.

(6) Except in special circumstances in which persuasive evidence exists, the following substantive premises will underlie the planning:

(a) Low-rise housing will be recommended, generally buildings no higher than three stories, and any buildings rising to four or five stories must be equipped with elevators.

(b) Financing techniques will be utilized wherever possible to encourage resident ownership, cooperatives and condominiums.

(c) Wherever possible, public low-income housing will not be concentrated but be scattered when achieved by new construction; in existing housing, the low-income families will be accommodated anonymously in housing serving a variety of income groups.

(d) The housing program will be designed to provide decent, desirable accommodations for Woodlawn residents, but especially for families with children. Typical Woodlawn residents include single men and women living alone; childless married couples, young and old; couples with children where one spouse works; couples with children where both parents work; families with only one parent; families dependent on welfare support.

(e) The housing program also will be designed to serve a widely diverse mixture of Woodlawn individuals and families residing in all parts of the community area.

(f) It is recognized that certain buildings will require clearance and other buildings will require a reduction in overcrowding. In these circumstances, the families affected will not be viewed as a displacement problem, i.e., as part of a relocation workload. Rather, the fact of displacement will provide the occasion for the development of an affirmative rehousing program to assist the affected families in improving their housing. The families thus affected will find that the process of displacement results in an improvement of their circumstances rather than a worsening, which has all too frequently been the unfortunate story of displacement to date.

(g) Other specific policy criteria of this type will be developed during the course of the undertaking.

Specific issues that must be handled by the environmental planning division initially, and subsequently by the Housing and Economic Development Corporation

PROGRAMMATIC COMPONENTS

during its operations, will be resolved according to the foregoing principles. Typical issues include the following:

(1) The use of such administrative instruments as Chicago Dwellings Association, rent supplements, 221 (d) (3), cooperatives, condominiums, etc., which can be brought to bear in dealing with the buildings referred to in the items immediately above with minimum reliance on public housing construction.

(2) The desirability of vest-pocket parks and play lots as well as the need for one or more larger scale parks.

(3) The possible use of the cemetery land for new construction, if the legal and political issues involved in removing the cemetery can be dealt with acceptably.

(4) The possible use of existing adjacent park areas for new construction pending the development of corresponding parks at other locations within the Woodlawn area.

(5) Exploring the possibility of enforcing codes on a community basis as well as of using code enforcement as a step in rehabilitation.

(6) Organizing groups of owners on a block or other unit basis to facilitate rehabilitation and property improvement.

(7) The organization of tenants on a building, block, and other unit basis to achieve property maintenance and improvement and facilitate the maintenance of building standards.

(8) A major re-examination of the welfare policy with respect to housing (see the financial assistance-income maintenance section). In lieu of the current practice of using receiverships and other legal instru-

ments to enforce decent housing practices by owners of buildings which include welfare tenants, there may be far more merit in developing an affirmative policy of housing families on welfare. Families on welfare will be provided housing assistance (including establishment of realistic rental allowances) to secure decent housing at the time the family goes on the welfare rolls. For those families now on the welfare rolls, assistance will be made available on a systematic case-by-case basis to assure that families are provided decent housing.

EDUCATION

The educational plan here envisioned grows out of the Woodlawn Experimental Schools Project (WESP) now in progress in three schools. The plan assumes that the goal at the outset must be the creation of a social and organizational "climate" in which fundamental change can take place in the operation and performance of the Woodlawn schools. It is our belief that basic change and improvement in inner-city education will require as necessary preliminary conditions two major steps:

First, the social and organizational climate of the schools must be transformed to one that emphasizes the dignity of the students, enhances their self-respect, and reduces the problem of alienation of community youth and adults from the schools.

Second, the schools must assume an effective coordinating role in the provision of services and resources needed by the child in his life outside the school.

Elaborating upon this coordinating role, Morris Janowitz (1968) has observed that:

PROGRAMMATIC COMPONENTS

To state that the school becomes the coordinating institution in the lives of its youngsters does not imply that it manages their total life space. It does not mean that the school directs the local health agency, the social agency, or the police in the immediate environment. It means that the requirements of the school serve as the stimulus for insuring relevant policy and practices by all these agencies. In particular, the school and the teacher become the central locus for all information about its students.[2]

Our belief in the need for these two major steps arises both from the sentiments voiced by Woodlawn residents and from the conclusions of scholars who have studied the problems of urban education in depth.[3]

Recent analysis[4] and experience suggests that piecemeal attacks upon the problems of inner-city education such as efforts focused upon curriculum reform, compensatory education, the application of educational technology, or combinations of such strategies will not bring about the desired broad-scale change and improvement. Thus, the WESP has undertaken a comprehensive approach, concentrating upon the creation of new roles and relationships which will require and produce significant changes of behavior on the part of all concerned—students, parents, school personnel, and other community members.[5] In this approach, the creation of the desired attitudes and relationships is viewed as more important than the specific programs initally undertaken to improve the schools. The focus of this effort is upon the development of "mutually helping relationships" among all involved as a principle means to open up communication, improve interpersonal relationships, and create a new, expanded, and positive social climate. This focus seeks to maximize student, parent, and community responsibility and involvement in the total educational process through such means as older students tutoring younger ones, community residents working as teacher aides and school-community representatives, and participation on citizen boards concerned with the schools. We recognize that the desired changes of behavior will not be easily accomplished and that the process may bring about conflict from time to time. Indeed, the experience to date of the WESP supports these expectations. However, what is at stake here clearly outweighs such considerations.

Through community discussions, study and analysis of the Woodlawn educational system in terms of modern educational theory, we conclude that a reorganization of the system is necessary in order to meet the needs of the different age groups of students. Beginning with the critically important creation of a comprehensive preschool program, we recommend in turn that the elementary schools be converted to primary schools serving kindergarten through grade 5, that two middle schools for grades 6 through 8 be built, and that the program of the high school be reconstructed through the development of a modern and relevant curriculum in which academic and vocational goals are seen as interdependent. In addition, we recommend the creation of a fluid schools system as an innovative means of increasing the penetration of the educational program into the community, thereby increasing the availability of educational services and, hopefully, reaching a segment of the population not now being served adequately or appropriately. Finally, we call for the creation of a Cultural and Language Arts Center to serve as a co-

PROGRAMMATIC COMPONENTS

ordinating center for adult education and, again on a coordinated basis, to make available the resources of modern educational technology to school children and adults.

The planning and participation structure of the proposed educational system for Woodlawn (see Chart 7) will provide for maximum citizen responsibility through the following components:

(1) The Woodlawn Community Board For Urban Education Projects (WCB) is the governing body of the current experimental school district project and consists of twenty-one members with seven representatives each from the Chicago Board of Education, The Woodlawn Organization, and the University of Chicago. Action by the board requires a consensus of all three groups. This board, or some modification of it as experience may suggest, will constitute the community's principal school system policy board. It will continue to carry out its two primary functions: (a) to review, discuss (and, in some cases, initiate) and prepare recommendations for policies and projects in urban education which will directly affect the children, adults, and community organization of Woodlawn; and (b) to provide a channel of communication between the projects and the larger institutions represented on the Woodlawn Community Board.

(2) The Advisory Planning Council will endeavor to make the Woodlawn educational program as comprehensive as possible through the development of a detailed program for inclusion of the Woodlawn parochial schools in the Model Cities program.

(3) Special Project Boards. The Preschool, Fluid Schools, and Cultural and Language Arts Center pro-

grams will each have an advisory board composed of community residents, professionals in applicable areas, and staff members of the given program. Each advisory board will be functionally responsible to the Woodlawn Community Board.

(4) The Woodlawn Organization Schools' Committee will continue to provide for the solicitation and consolidation of the views of the parent councils and other area residents on community educational policies and programs, as well as provision of community recommendations, to the Woodlawn Community Board.

(5) Parent councils will be organized around neighborhood schools and will solicit participation of parents and students in evaluating the status of the Model Cities' education program and provide a forum where parents, teachers, and administrators can clarify school and community aims.

The overall objectives constituting the goals of the total educational program for the people, young and old, of Woodlawn are the following: (1) to make education relevant to the recipient's environment and to his future; (2) to increase his sense of mastery over his environment and destiny; (3) to increase ability to learn and adapt; (4) to produce significant improvements in achievement in language arts and quantitative skills; (5) to meet the needs of different age groups; and (6) to identify and aid "excluded" and "exceptional" students.

The following brief descriptions of the proposed programs are intended to be suggestive of the general character of the Woodlawn Model Cities' education plan.

PROGRAMMATIC COMPONENTS

Preschool Centers

The ultimate goal of the preschool plan is to provide a quality program of half-day instruction and half-day care for the approximately 2,000 three and four-year olds in Woodlawn. This program should be operated twelve months a year in small centers to be located throughout the community in either rented, renovated or specially constructed facilities. The number, size, and location of centers to be built or rented will be determined during the first and second years of the program.

For maximum individualization, class size will be held to fifteen children per teacher and teacher aide. In order to give each child a feeling of security and belonging, he will be assigned at admission time to a small "family" consisting of several children of different ages and one staff member who will be responsible for their welfare throughout the day. This staff member will also keep comprehensive records on the child, including relevant features of his home situation, and will help coordinate needed services for the child and his family.

The preschool program will utilize multi-age grouping and will be organized to permit flexibility and creative use of space, time, materials, and resources by the staff. Every effort will be made to enlist, as members of the staff, residents of Woodlawn. In this connection, a major thrust of the program will be directed toward parent education and involvement, with school-community representatives assisting the teachers and teacher aides in establishing close and continuing relationships with parents.

By the end of the first year, plans should be completed

for the rental and construction of facilities needed to serve approximately one-half of the target population. During the second year a pilot program will be operated, construction will begin, and planning will continue for the rental and construction of the remaining facilities needed to serve the total population.

Primary Schools

The main thrusts of the primary program will be directed toward (1) improving relationships between teachers and students and between parents and school personnel, and (2) improving student achievement in basic skills. The development of close and mutually helping relationships among all concerned will be fostered by a number of means, such as collaborative study and definition of the roles and relationships between and among administrators, teachers, teacher aides, community representatives, parents, and students; participation on parent councils; and the development of a tutoring program using older students and adults as both volunteer and paid tutors.

Among the more direct and specific approaches to the improvement of achievement are measures taken to promote the individualization of instruction. Here our plan calls for the placement of a teacher aide in every classroom, reduction of class size to twenty-five pupils, and creation of a coordinated program of tutoring. In addition, teachers will be urged to use new ideas and approaches to meet the needs of their students. An educational fund will be established from which teachers may draw to furnish materials for instruction innovation. It will no longer be necessary for committed teachers and concerned parents to pay for needed supplies out of

PROGRAMMATIC COMPONENTS

CHART 7.

PLANNING AND PARTICIPATION STRUCTURE - WOODLAWN COMMUNITY SCHOOLS

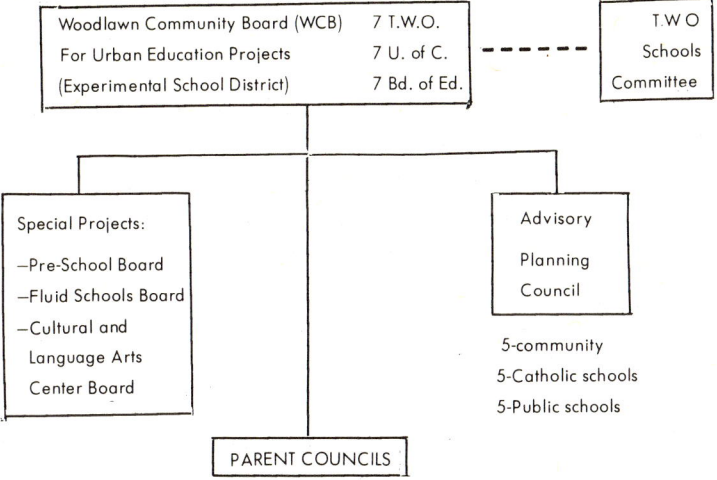

145

their own pockets. Another innovative step to promote individualization and achievement will be the coordinated use of the resources of modern educational technology (including "talking typewriters") to be housed in the proposed Cultural and Language Arts Center, which will serve both youngsters and adults. Finally, the development of a more effective instructional program will be pursued through in-service training of teachers and teacher aides utilizing the leadership of consultants and two teaching-learning specialists who will be hired on a full-time basis.

The planning period for the conversion of the Woodlawn elementary schools into primary schools serving kindergarten through 5th grade will begin at the start of the second year of the Model Cities plan so that the conversion of three schools can be undertaken during the third year in coordination with the beginning of the operation of the first of the two middle schools to be constructed. During the third year, plans will be laid for the conversion of three more elementary schools in coordination with the opening of the second middle school.

Middle Schools

To replace the upper grade center program, we propose to build two school-within-a-school complexes as middle schools to serve the approximately 2,400 students in grades 6 through 8 in Woodlawn. Each complex will enroll 1,200 students and will consist of four academic houses surrounding a resource center "hub." Each academic house will serve 300 students with a staff of fifteen teachers; ten to twelve teacher aides; and supporting specialists, counselors, community representatives and clerical help. Each complex will include space for individual study, counseling offices, recreation facilities, and modern shops and laboratories.

To promote personal and social development, each student will be a member of a "home-base" group led by a team consisting of a teacher, a teacher aide or a community representative, and a counselor. The regular meetings of the "home-base" group will be used flexibly for talks with individual students or small groups of students with similar problems or tasks and for the planning and execution of group activities. The team leading the group will continue the record keeping and coordination of services for each student begun in the preschool program, will place emphasis upon helping each student understand himself as an individual with personal needs and shared social responsibilities, and will provide career counseling for each student.

Hyde Park High School

A principal part of the effort to improve the performance of Hyde Park High School will be directed toward developing a new curriculum in which general and vocational education are integrated and seen as inter dependent. Vocational preparation will be used to make general education concrete and understandable while general education will point up the vocational implications of all education. Employment preparation and occupational information courses will constitute a central component of the curriculum. Vocational and college counseling will be regularly available to all students. A college preparatory program, seen as one component of the overall career preparation program, will be offered to those students interested in college or paraprofessional training. The high school will work in close coordination with the Career Vocational Institute (elsewhere discussed) in developing job training, work-study, counseling, and job placement programs. The "Homework Helper" program, in which high school students will be paid to tutor younger students, will be one part of this total effort.

To strengthen the instructional program, teacher aides and additional teachers will be hired, thereby reducing class size and the teacher-pupil ratio. The ratio of students to teachers (not including teacher aides) should not exceed twenty-to-one. In the general effort to individualize instruction, the potentialities of the educational technology to be made available at the Cultural and Language Arts Center will be tapped. Indeed, the emphasis of the instructional program will be upon the development of independent study and continuous learning skills. For a number of students this may well require, as a preliminary step, an intensive remedial program focused upon basic language arts and quantitative skills. Even here, however, an emphasis will be placed upon showing students how they can pursue knowledge independently and continuously.

The Fluid Schools

The fluid schools constitute a major creative, constructive, and revolutionary response to the delivery of educational services, since they might well provide quality education, adapted to the needs of school dropouts in a setting and manner most conducive and receptive to the population sought to be served.

The fluid schools follow the health model. Classrooms serving each educational programmatic component—

preschool, primary, middle and high—will be located outside of formal school buildings in single rooms or in limited numbers of rooms in houses, apartment buildings, industrial establishments, recreation centers, hospitals, and like structures. It will be possible to secure an entire education through this device, or an education for a given grade level, or for a limited number of grades— with more emphasis placed on content and subject matter achievement than on formal grade level achievement. These fluid schools opportunities will be related to the outreach facilities (the Pads), which are the point of individual, family, and parent contact on the range of human problems (jobs, legal assistance, health aid, and the like). Thus, education will be incorporated as yet another ingredient via the instrument of the fluid schools.

The fluid schools, while using professional teachers, will also rely heavily on teaching by trained parents, older peer group students, factory foremen, clinic directors, and other non-educational professionals. Students may be expected to attend formal classes in conventional school buildings one day a week where they will have access to special facilities not available in the fluid schools.

In sum, the school is brought to the people—the residents, the parents, and the students—the consumers of educational services. The need to alter radically the pattern of delivery of services may be as important in the education area as it is in health, social service, and other subject areas. It is incumbent upon the educational establishment (as it is on all other professional establishments) to refashion itself according to the needs and goals of the users of services rather than to demand accommodation on the part of the user himself.

WOODLAWN'S MODEL CITIES PLAN

Cultural and Language Arts Center

The Cultural and Language Arts Center is proposed as a multi-purpose facility to offer a varied program for young and old intended to fill a number of gaps which now exist in the cultural and educational life of Woodlawn. The Center will have three principal objectives: (1) to coordinate, augment, and improve existing adult education programs; (2) to offer individualized learning experiences utilizing the resources of educational technology; and (3) to develop, coordinate, and sponsor cultural activities, especially in the area of Afro-American Arts and humanities.

The Center will be centrally located in the community, perhaps separate from any of the now existing schools in the area. Physically it will resemble a modern learning resource center, with a series of listening rooms, twenty "talking typewriters," and supporting audio-visual equipment and materials. A staff of educational media specialists, reading specialists, teachers, and teacher aides will assist persons using the facilities. The nature of the equipment and program will be such that virtually all age and ability groups will be readily accommodated and served.

The Center will be operated fourteen hours a day, five days a week, and twelve months a year with the staff working in two shifts each day. To make the Center more attractive during its summer operation it will be air-conditioned. The Center will be administered and coordinated by a director and a citizens' advisory board.

PROGRAMMATIC COMPONENTS

Recreation Center

To augment the recreation facilities available through the Cultural and Language Arts Center and the park and school systems, there would be constructed at least one recreation center in the target area. The center will include facilities not appropriate to the smaller, scattered sites, such as (1) a swimming pool, (2) a skating rink, (3) a gymnasium, (4) an indoor court for badminton, (5) table tennis facilities, (6) stage space for cultural programming, (7) meeting rooms, and (8) tennis courts.

The construction of a center in the Parkside and Essex communities to the south of the target area would be encouraged to house similar facilities, which would be available to the neighboring communities. Local adult and teenage employees and volunteers will be engaged to operate these centers.

HOUSING AND ECONOMIC DEVELOPMENT AND EMPLOYMENT

The programs envisioned for the Housing and Economic Development Corporation (HED) are broadly comprehensive and, at the same time, diverse. They include employment preparation with training programs embodied in a Career Vocational Institute (CVI), job development through the attraction of new businesses to an industrial park, black entrepreurship, and community ventures through the mechanism of a small business service program and housing improvement through the associated programs of the Core and HED.

Chart 8 depicts these program emphases in relation to program goals and approaches, earlier discussed. Housing has not been included in this diagram, nor will it be treated in the following sections on "priorities and feasibility," since programs in this field originate in the environmental planning section of Core and for this reason need to be justified and analyzed much more broadly than in terms of an economic rationale. However, the mechanism for effectuating these programs the HED, and a section on housing will follow the discussions on career preparation, an industrial park, and small business.

PROGRAMMATIC COMPONENTS

CHART 8. PROGRAM GOALS AND APPROACHES FOR EMPLOYMENT, HOUSING, AND ECONOMIC DEVELOPMENT

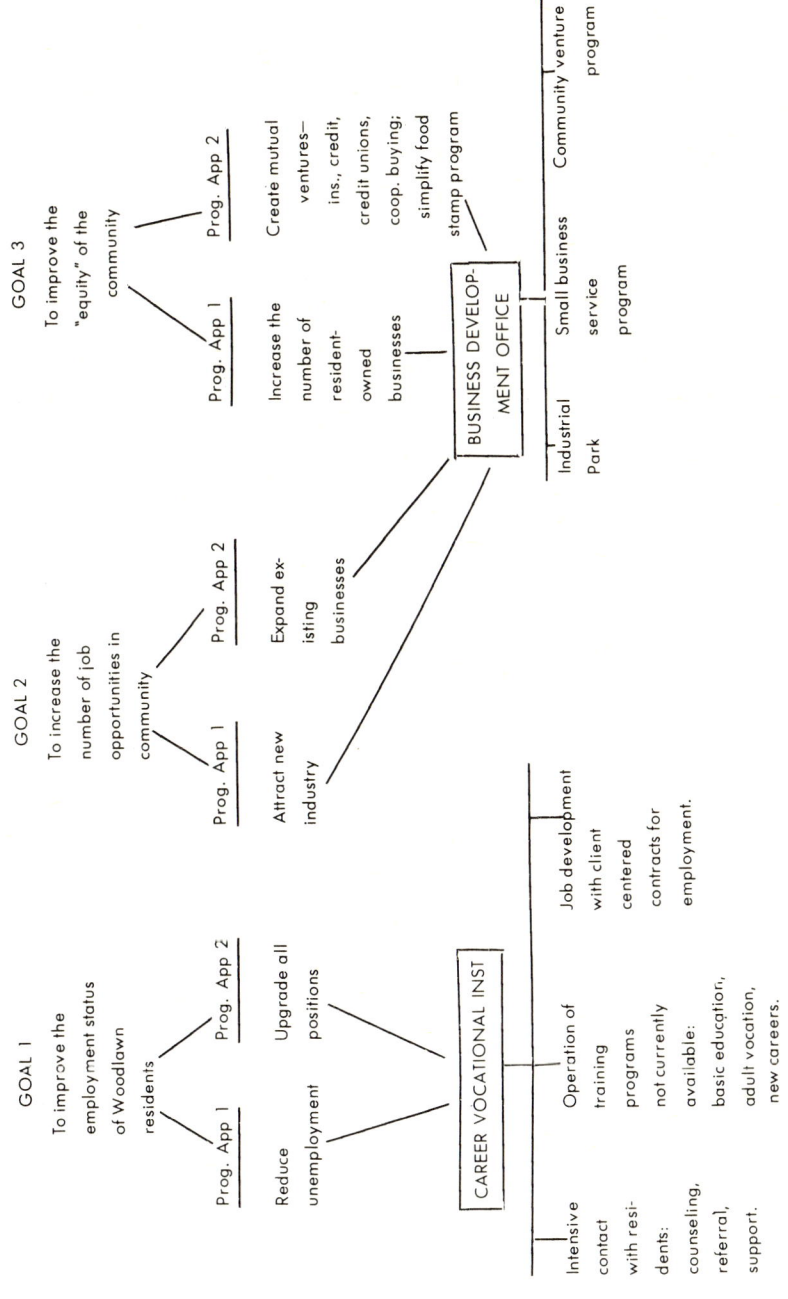

153

WOODLAWN'S MODEL CITIES PLAN

Priorities

In a purely economic sense it is hard to justify goals 2 and 3, shown in Chart 8, i.e., the creation of more jobs within Woodlawn and the development of more community equity. Both of these goals have to be justified on social or political grounds. Having stated this proviso, we will turn to an analysis of possible income effects, primarily from the worker preparation programs, and leave the more complex subject of evaluating the total utility of various goals for a later section—after we have developed all of the costs and benefits.

One technique for gauging the potential payoffs present in the employment area is to disaggregate the income differential between Woodlawn and Chicago workers into the unemployment and occupational position components. (See Table 1.)

The relationships can best be developed by a series of conditional statements:

(1) If unemployment were eliminated and the workers received the average income of already employed workers in the community, then overall income would increase by the amount of unemployment reduction. Assuming a current rate of 15% unemployment, this would mean an increase in income of 12% if unemployment were dropped to the national standard of 3%; or an income improvement of 9% if unemployment were dropped to the rate prevailing for whites in urban neighborhoods, namely 6%.

(2) If Woodlawn workers already employed received the same wages as Chicago workers generally, then overall income would increase by 22% for men and 9% for women. Essentially, the technique is one of applying

total or white income figures to the Woodlawn distribution and comparing it against actual income.

(3) If Woodlawn workers, already employed, enjoyed the same occupational position as Chicago workers generally and received wages generally paid for that work, income would be increased 45% for men and 30% for women.

Quite significantly, the median family income in 1967 for the city of Chicago was 48% higher than for Woodlawn, according to the figures of the Hospital Planning Council. This correspondence suggests that most of the difference in median family income between Woodlawn and the rest of Chicago has been explained.

On the basis of the above figures, one might readily conclude that more important payoffs are to be realized from a program aimed at upgrading rather than reducing unemployment. However, such is not the case when viewed on a per capita basis. The economic gain to an individual from obtaining employment at $4,000 per year is substantially more than could be gained by an individual as a result of upgrading. It is true that upgrading may benefit many more individuals, but the individual utility is not as great. Moreover, there are important social reasons for giving high priority to the elimination of unemployment. Half of the total group is made up of youth, and community leaders desire to give strong emphasis to the objective of engaging the community's younger generation in productive activity.

Feasibility of Achieving Results

In some respects, the elimination of unemployment would seem to be the easiest to achieve since individuals ought to be able to be placed on jobs quite quickly.

While in some cases this is true, in many instances the progress is long and arduous—the term "hard core" is not without relevance. However, the ease with which a person can be upgraded is often also overstated. Statistics only measure whether he completed the course and obtained a job afterward and not the caliber of the job.

One of the important factors affecting feasibility is the ability of individuals to be upgraded or to secure a job if they are unemployed. Approximately one-third of the workers in Woodlawn have a high-school diploma and this percentage is increasing rapidly: the drop-out rate at Hyde Park High School is approximately 30%, and national figures recently released indicate that Negro men aged twenty to twenty-four have a high-school completion rate of over 50%.[6]

When educational attainment is examined for different occupations, it is found that only the professional manager and the craft occupations demonstrate a high-school diploma as a prevalent attribute.

A more conclusive analysis is shown in Table 1 which for the city of Chicago asks the question: If education and age perform for Negroes in the same way that they do for whites, what would the occupational position look like? One can note from Tables 1 and 2 that a considerable disparity exists between the expected and actual positions, especially in the better occupations.

The general thrust of the above has been to demonstrate that more than enough education is present in Woodlawn to overcome the occupational distribution differential that exists. Just how much should be spent on such a program depends upon considerations such as the probability of success, the time horizon, and the money costs involved. Some of these considerations are summarized in Table 2.

Career Preparation Within the HED

The needs of general education and vocational training cannot be separated in a community such as Woodlawn where the vast majority of youth go directly from school into the labor market rather than continue their formal education at the college level. It is necessary to integrate vocational education and career training, at all levels, with education in the public schools of Woodlawn so that all persons, regardless of age or sex, are adequately prepared for careers suited to their needs, aptitudes, and interests. Career preparation will occur in three basic settings: (1) in the regular public school system, specifically, the schools of the Experimental District; (2) in a Career Vocational Institute (CVI), run by a separate board in the Housing and Economic Development Corporation (HED), and (3) in existing programs, including on-the-job training programs.

Within each setting, vocational education will be tailored to meet the individual's needs. This means that it may range from the teaching of general career orientations, to highly generalized basic skills, to specific entry skills. The objectives of education will be determined by the individual's needs: one person must be prepared for college, another for paraprofessional service, a third for immediate employment in industry. The placement of an individual in a specific educational program will be determined by his desires and abilities as ascertained by means of intake counseling, a function to be located within the CVI. The primary focus of adult education will

WOODLAWN'S MODEL CITIES PLAN

TABLE 1

EXPECTED VS. ACTUAL DISTRIBUTION
OF NEGRO EMPLOYMENT IN CHICAGO
(1960 REPRESENTATION)

	Expected Occupational Distribution of Chicago Male Negroes if their Education and Age Characteristics Acted in the Same Way as for Male Whites in the Central Cities	Actual Distribution of Chicago Male Negroes
Professional & Technical	6.6	2.9
Managerial & Office	8.9	1.9
Office & Clerical	8.0	9.6
Sales	7.2	1.7
Craft	21.8	9.9
Operator	24.4	26.4
Service	8.5	14.6
Laborer	7.7	14.3
Other not Reported	7.0	18.1
	100.0%	100.0%

PROGRAMMATIC COMPONENTS

TABLE 2

SUMMARY CONSIDERATIONS

	Reduced Unemployment	Increased Upgrading	More Jobs in Community	Local Ownership	Cooperative Association
BENEFITS	Increase Income 9-12%	Increase Income 40%	Some increase in employment	Success Symbol	Better Services
	Great utility to individual	Considerable utility to large number of people	Easier accessibility	$500 - 900,000 more income and some increase in employment	Community pride
	Considerable utility to community		Better connection between learning and earning		
FEASIBILITIES					
Probability of Success	85%	75%	40%	60%	30%
Time Horizon	6-9 months	1-2 years	3-5 years	1-year	2 years
Costs per Individual	$2,000	$3,000	----	$5,000	

be the CVI; youth education will, of course, continue to take place within the public school system. In order to achieve the highest degree of integration of educational services to young people, there must be the closest relationship between the CVI and Woodlawn Community Board for Urban Education (WCB).

The Three Settings of Career Preparation

The Public Schools. The school curriculum should be revised to meet the needs of the students, most of whom will not go on to college yet must be guaranteed adequate preparation for post-school entry into meaningful careers. Some type of career preparation should be a part of every student's educational experience; this does not mean, however, that the individual should be tailored to meet the needs of the labor market. On the contrary, the objective of vocational education should be the development of the individual—not his channeling into areas of short-run demand in the labor market. Employment preparation and occupational information courses should be given throughout the school program and at the high-school level should constitute a central feature of the curriculum. The following points are offered as guidelines for curriculum development:

(1) Occupational preparation begins at the elementary level with a realistic picture of work responsibility.

(2) Occupational preparation becomes more sophisticated at the upper-grade level with the addition of courses in economics and the initiation of vocational training.

(3) Occupational preparation should become more specific in high school, built around families of occupations or industries which are undergoing expansion.

Entry skills should be taught to those outside the college preparatory curriculum.

(4) Vocational testing, the evaluation of interests and aptitudes of the student, should begin in grade school and continue throughout high school.

(5) A college preparatory program should be offered to those students interested in college or in paraprofessional training. This does not imply a division between "academic" and "vocational" coursework, except at the skill-training level. Otherwise, vocational and general education will be integrated: vocational preparation will be used to make general education concrete and understandable; general education should point up the vocational implications of all education.[7]

(6) Vocational counseling should be regularly available to all students; placement can be provided by the Career Vocational Institute, described below.

(7) Job training and work-study, both publicly and privately funded, should be made available to students who desire the experience or who need the financial support. Work-experience programs, arranged by the school, would provide on-the-job skill training, preferably in growing sectors of the economy.

(8) Training and placement of students in paraprofessional positions, such as teachers' aides, welfare aides, etc., should be a part of the vocational curriculum. The paraprofessional program, which crosscuts the three settings, is discussed separately.

(9) Students should be encouraged to finish high school. This will in part be accomplished by the revision of curriculum along lines suggested in this proposal, which will make the high-school experience more meaningful to the career interests of the student.

(10) Teaching innovations such as team teaching and

problem-orientation should be developed that reflect the integration of vocational and general education.

(11) Programs designed to enable the former drop-out to finish high school should be offered; work-study and work-experience programs should be made available to such persons as necessary.

Career Vocational Institute (CVI). The CVI is a new facility designed to centralize and integrate employment preparation services for members of the Woodlawn community. It will efficiently provide a wide range of services for persons of all ages, sexes, and backgrounds: the hard-core unemployed adult, totally lacking in skill-training; the high-school graduate, seeking paraprofessional experience; the high-school drop-out; the ADC mother—all will be served at the CVI. The emphasis of CVI training will be career preparation: basic educational deficiencies will be remedied, knowledge of career possibilities offered, and specific skills of a wide variety taught. Yet the individual's training program would be tailored to his needs; those desiring extensive institutional training will be served along with those desiring immediate placement in on-the-job skill training programs. In general, basic education will underlie all vocational training at the CVI, probably beginning before the initiation of vocational training and continuing throughout the training program. As in the public school curriculum, described above, a primary goal will be the integration of basic general education and vocational training in a program of career preparation.

The CVI will be established separately in the HED and be governed by a specially designated board which will seek to facilitate coordination between vocational and general aspects of education as well as guarantee

PROGRAMMATIC COMPONENTS

community control over the community-oriented facility. (See Chart 9.) It is recommended that the CVI Board consist of three persons from The Woodlawn Organization (one of whom it is urged be a young adult), three persons from the University of Chicago, and three persons from the Woodlawn Community Board. This board, hereafter referred to as the CVI Board, would periodically report to the HED, to which it is legally responsible, as well as to the WCB; it would, however, have responsibility for setting policy and making operational decisions regarding the functioning of the CVI. The director of the CVI will be chosen by the CVI Board; thereafter, he will sit on the Board as a member.

A nonvoting advisory group will attend regular sessions of the CVI Board. While the exact composition of this group will be determined by the CVI Board, it should consist of the following members: person(s) from Illinois State Employment Service, representing the Department of Labor; person(s) from The Woodlawn Organization, specialized in vocational training programs; person(s) from industry, drawn from those corporations that have expressed a willingness to train and employ the innercity, unskilled Negro poor; person(s) from the Board of Vocational Education; and person(s) from the University of Chicago, both from the divisions (especially the Business School) and the administration (especially Personnel). The director of the CVI would have responsibility for the ongoing operations of the Institute. He would be aided by two supervisors and an administrative assistant, the latter responsible for staff operations.

The trainee may come to the CVI by any one of several avenues: in active quest of a job or of upgrading or recruited from a street corner or poolroom by a CVI staff counselor. Through discussions with the intake counselor he determines which training program, or what combination of programs, is best suited to his needs and abilities. He may be placed in a basic education class, a skill class, or a paraprofessional training program; he may be placed in an on-the-job training program or directly on a job. If the application presents special problems—legal, proper placement, etc.—their dispostion will be decided by a review panel consisting of the director, the two supervisors, appropriate members of the counseling staff, and a legal consultant (if necessary). As the trainee proceeds through the program and onto a job, he receives close counseling by a member of the counseling staff; followup counseling after placement is realized will also be offered. CVI personnel in charge of job-development—the director, the field supervisor, and several counselors—will coordinate their activities with those of the intake counselors: every CVI trainee must be guaranteed a position immediately upon graduation from the Institute. The job-development staff will work with legal advisors, as necessary, in order to obtain openings in industry, union memberships, apprenticeship programs, etc.

The CVI will have the following characteristics:

(1) Long-range public financing.

(2) Service to all persons, of both sexes, of all economic groups.

(3) MDTA - level stipends for all CVI students over 17.

(4) HEW and Labor Department officials and funds will be brought together.

(5) Available on a 16-18 hour daily basis, 7 days a week, 52 weeks a year.

(6) Curriculum tailored to meet the needs of the

trainee, covering the entire occupational spectrum—from managerial and professional to skilled industrial labor.

(7) Will not supplant high-school education: safeguards against dropping out of high school to join the CVI could include a 17-year minimum age restriction on stipend receipt, as well as restricting entry to persons who had been out of school a specified minimum amount of time (such as one full semester).

(8) A certificate or diploma should be given at the completion of training.

(9) A General Equivalency Degree (GED) should be available for those who desire it and successfully complete the requirements.

(10) A public information service should be run to inform non-CVI trainees in Woodlawn about careers in growth areas; this could be run through the office of the director by his administrative assistant.

(11) A direct relationship with the community Core Corporation; the outreach facilities, the Pad, and the day-care and preschool centers.

(12) The New Careers concept in developing indigenous staff should be an objective.

(13) Insofar as the professional sector is the fastest growing sector of the economy, it is hoped that eventually the New Careers program would become the major thrust of CVI.

(14) Basic education, under the CVI, will include not only communication and computation skills, but also work in career orientation, labor market trends, Negro history, presentation of self in job interview and job situations, etc. Insofar as possible, basic education courses will be rendered concrete and understandable through a vocational reference.

(15) Vocational training will include the teaching of

skill families as well as specific entry skills; the latter may often be learned best on-the-job, by special arrangement with the employer.

(16) In conjunction with the high school, the CVI will arrange for work-study and work-experience programs and will provide college opportunity counseling.

(17) Imaginative teaching innovations—including machine teaching and team teaching—will be employed where possible by the CVI.

The CVI will be housed in a modern facility designed to meet the needs of the Institute. It is hoped that the facility could be located in close proximity with the Woodlawn schools, particularly Hyde Park High School.

Existing Programs, Including On-The-Job Training (OJT). Existing programs, both public (ISES, OEO programs) and private (Midway Technical, other schools), provide a useful service to many who desired employment or upgrading; it is felt, however, that they fail to reach those whose needs are greatest. These people can only be reached by radical departures, beginning at the earliest stages of education; such approaches are described above. Nonetheless, the utility of existing programs is recognized. It is therefore recommended that the referral service, operating out of CVI, maintain comprehensive and up-to-date files of existing public and private programs both in the Greater Woodlawn area and in the city as a whole. Those persons whose needs are best filled by referral to existing programs will be channeled by the referral service into these programs.

OJT will be undertaken where appropriate. The CVI referral service will place people directly in OJT positions, if this is felt to be in the best interests of the appli-

PROGRAMMATIC COMPONENTS

cants. Work-experience programs—and, to a lesser degree, work-study programs—have aspects of OJT which have been previously discussed; the public school will serve as the referral agency, aided by the CVI. OJT will also characterize a substantial part of the New Careers training. CVI job-development personnel would have the responsibility for developing the OJT positions.

Special Programs

Two special programs which crosscut the three settings of training described above are summarized below (Aides and New Careers):

Aides. Aides are subprofessionals (medical, teacher, social service, and legal) who, it is felt, will increasingly assume responsibilities presently performed by professionals. The criteria for establishing aide positions are threefold: that they benefit the trainee in opening career possibilities; that they benefit the community in providing needed services best performed by local citizens; and that they relieve the professional from the burden of work that does not require his skills and training.

Aides will be trained at the CVI to the extent necessary, although OJT is to be encouraged in this program; many positions require little advance preparation outside of basic skills (nurse's aides, for example, presently receive only three weeks of formal training at Billings Hospital). The balance between institutional and on-the-job training will be determined by the nature of the position and the qualifications of the individual. Those aides who are interested could enroll in the New Careers program, described below. The New Career office, set up within the CVI, will deal with the Aide Program; this office would have responsibility for all aide trainees, whether they were being trained under New Careers, under other CVI programs, or directly on-the-job. One of the responsibilities of this office would be to thoroughly investigate aide programs elsewhere, focusing on the possibility of career development from aide positions in the various fields; supportive and upgrading programs would be developed as necessary.

New Careers for the Residents of Woodlawn. The New Careers program for paraprofessional and professional training will operate out of the CVI. The program will be open to anyone, but basic education courses must be given to those who have deficiencies before other coursework begins; a high-school equivalency degree will be offered. Persons who oppose institutional training leading to the equivalency degree should be referred to other training programs under the CVI or directly to OJT. Participants will work as aides in various public agencies and private industries, with the intention of moving up to a higher position; they will receive institutional educational training, work experience, and a full salary. The program will be open only to persons over eighteen years of age. Four hours a day will be spent on the job and four hours in the classroom and studying. College courses in local colleges, leading either to the B.A. (four years) or A.A. (two years), will be the final degree a person could receive in this program, although a special certificate could be given to persons who successfully completed a training course without achieving the college degree. New Careers thus differs from other CVI training programs in that it involves extensive institutional training, in some cases of a fairly general nature, leading to a subprofessional or professional career; a college degree is the ultimate objective of the program. New Career Aides would work in public agencies (teacher aides, social service aides, medical aides, legal aides, police aides, recreation aides), in private organizations (Urban League, universities), and in industry (computer operations, business administration, management, clerical, some skilled labor positions). The agency or firm must provide useful and meaningful work for the aide during the training period, and guarantee him employment at a higher wage level than that received during training upon successful completion of the program. If union membership is required for certain positions, efforts should be made to ensure that there will be no racial bars when the applicant has fulfilled the requirements for membership. Salary arrangements will be made with the employing agency or firm; in general, they will be scaled to increase over the years of training with $100 per week as the base salary in the first year. Government funds will cover all salary costs the first year, with the agency or firm assuming one-third of the cost in second and subsequent years. The length of training will vary with the individual and the position being trained for. Counseling and other supportive services will be provided by the CVI. The New Careers program will be administered by a separate office within the CVI comprised of a coordinator and several assistants responsible for job development, unions, career-in-aide development (and general research), and counseling.

Related Proposals

(1) An Office of Information should be established within the administrative offices of the director of the CVI to gather and make available information on labor market conditions, occupational trends, changing population and employment characteristics of the community, information on other public and private training programs, and comprehensive data on all CVI trainees.

(2) Evaluation will be contracted out to an appropriate firm.

(3) In order to enable mothers to take advantage of CVI programs, or obtain employment directly, extensive day-care facilities will be established within the community. These centers must be of sufficient scale to free many mothers for training and employment; furthermore, they must emphasize the employment of local people as aides, where possible. Private support should be sought from the firms employing mothers released for work by the Centers.

(4) Improved transportation to major centers of work would facilitate residents in obtaining employment in areas distant from Woodlawn. This matter should be explored by the Housing and Economic Development Corporation, discussed elsewhere.

(5) The legal work of the CVI will be undertaken by special arrangement with the Law Division within the Core.

PROGRAMMATIC COMPONENTS

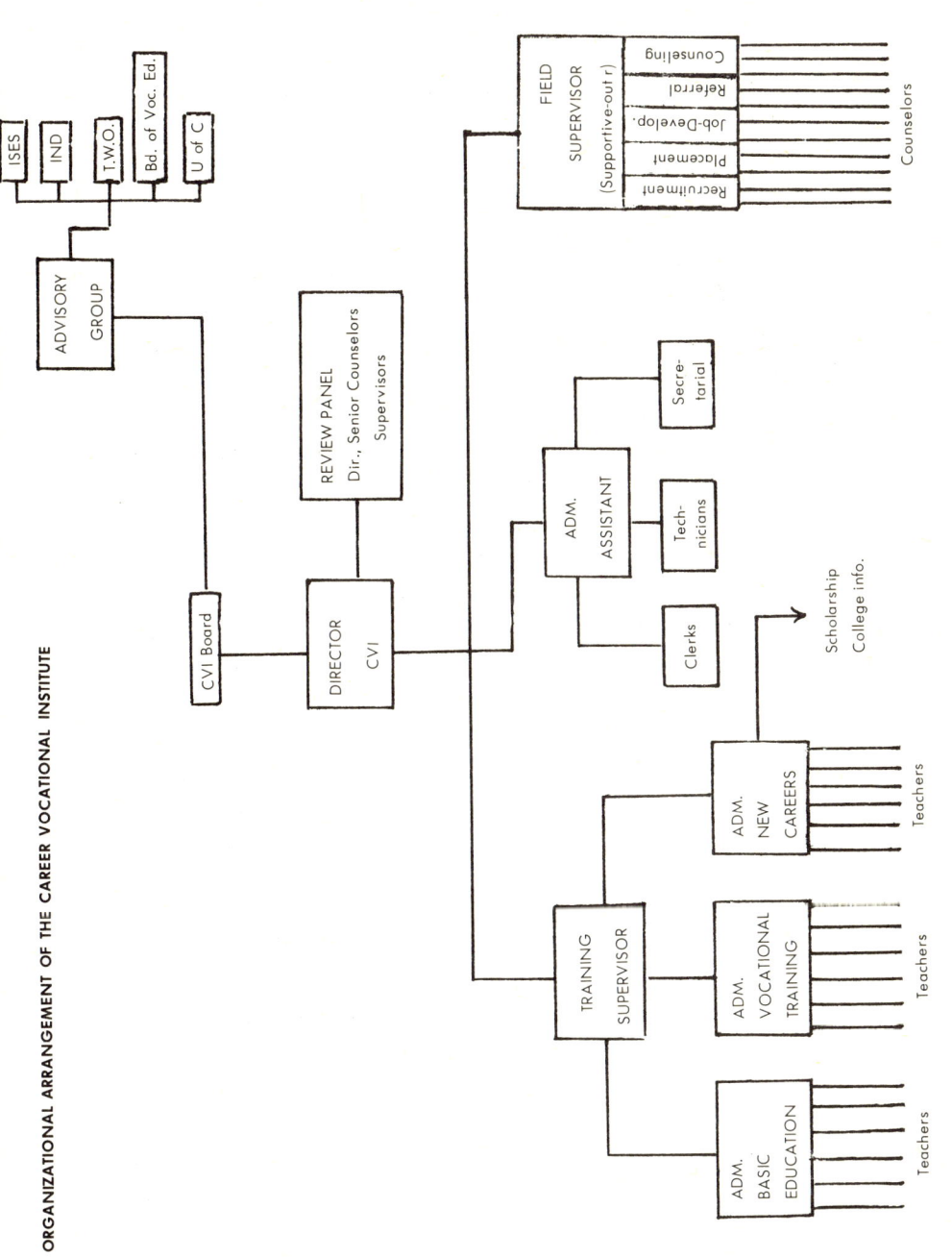

CHART 9. ORGANIZATIONAL ARRANGEMENT OF THE CAREER VOCATIONAL INSTITUTE

Housing and Economic Development Functions of the HED

Industrial Park

The HED will have the responsibility for attracting new industry to an industrial park. It should seek ways to interest industry in the community and convince it to settle there once interest has been aroused. It should know all the advantages and disadvantages for movement of industry into various target-area sites and devise means to cure or circumvent the disadvantageous factors.

Industrial site-seekers are very concerned about hard, cold facts such as chemical analyses of industrial water, tax assessment ratios, and foundation subsoil qualities. To answer these questions, the HED will need to do a lot of intensive research. It will also have to provide information on the following subjects most often raised by industrial site-seekers: (1) description of industrial sites and buildings, (2) labor supply and living conditions, (3) transportation facilities, (4) power, fuel, and water, (5) raw materials, (6) business climate, and (7) taxes and cost of land.

As one major advantage, Woodlawn offers industry a readily available labor supply which can easily be tapped. A representative of Commonwealth Edison's Industrial Development Department has stated that many new industries locating in the northwest suburbs are having problems recruiting plant labor. While his organization has been diligently attempting to persuade companies to relocate to the southern part of Chicago, they are reluctant to do so because of concern for plant and personnel security, and, as a result, choose the suburbs even though labor is not readily available. As an alternative, it was suggested that a plan whereby the community or community organization purchases a site and erects a building with leasing available to an industrial concern might be very attractive. This would be so because the company would feel that the community has a demonstrated interest in the plant's security.

The industrial activities can be summarized in outline form:

(1) Recruitment of industry (light manufacturing), such as IBM, camera, electronics, garment, food-processing and packaging (which could be tied in with a southern Negro producers' cooperative), glasscutting, dry cleaning and processing, data processing, computing, shoe manufacture, etc. Make contact with large nonindustrial corporations in hopes of inducing them to locate branches in Woodlawn. Among those that might be approached are automotive dealerships, servicing facilities (Volkswagon, Ford, etc.).

(2) Investigate and promote the concentration of light industry in an industrial park. A probable location for such park is between Stony Island and Blackstone, and 71st and 73rd Streets. This would be analogous to an inner-city development corporation.

(3) Negotiate with big corporations the possibility of establishing and supporting a large Negro-owned business by agreeing to purchase a certain amount of its products. Several Negro suppliers could thus be supported. (A similar agreement was worked out between FIGHT and XEROX in Rochester.)

Small Business Service Program

In general, the purpose of a small business development office (see Chart 10 on the following page) is to put the pieces of black business development together. As previously stated, individuals are available, capital can be obtained, and viable business opportunities can be defined. What is lacking is the ability to fuse these elements together. The small business development office is designed to do this by the means described below.

Program. The activities of the organization can be dealt with in the typical sequence through which a project will pass.

Business Opportunity Analysis. An important function of the office will be to identify important business opportunities, either those already under way in the community or those that might be introduced. Such an analysis will entail an inventory of important economic needs not being presently filled in existing businesses. For example, residents have indicated that credit and insurance are inadequately serviced and these areas might provide important economic opportunities. In the same vein, suggestions have been made about increasing the recreational facilities in the community via a skating rink and a country club—both of these might be run on a for-profit basis.

PROGRAMMATIC COMPONENTS

CHART 10

ORGANIZATION OF THE
BUSINESS DEVELOPMENT OFFICE

DIRECTOR

Community Relations	Bus. Oppor. Analysis	Project Directors	Training & Consult. Services Coordinator
2 people fund-raising talent search	2 staff specialists	4 persons each handle 10 accounts	1 person acts as go-between, contracting special programs with educational institutions

The analysis section will also investigate the areas of retailing that are relevant, given the income profile of the community and projections for the next five to ten years. Professor Brian J. L. Berry has done an important piece of work on the mortality rates of different retail categories with special attention to the south side of Chicago. This study will be an important input into defining the categories of activity in which business ownership has a good chance of succeeding. One such area may be that of food retailing: while the profit margins are small, food is nevertheless an important item and a number of businesses have been quite successful.

Recently, several white retailers on 63rd Street, especially in the dry cleaning and shoe businesses have shown interest in selling their stores to area residents. If analysis demonstrated that these were viable business opportunities, the office might help secure the talent.

The attracting of new businesses into the community is perhaps even more important than the restructuring of existing businesses. For example, the University of Chicago is showing interest in having some of its needs supplied by black entrepreneurs from Woodlawn. One concrete possibility is that of mimeographing, in which with a modest amount of capital a business could be established to serve some of the University's needs. Other examples are livery service and laundry supply.

The latter also relates to the new Veterans' Administration Hospital and the type of services that it will require, with the possibility that the community might supply many of them. On a wider basis, large Chicago corporations might be willing to sponsor local businesses on either a partnership basis or on a spin-off arrangement. This is the model followed by Xerox in the establishment of FIGHT in Rochester and by Western

Electric in the establishment of a wooden-crate fabricator in Chicago.

Community Contact (Talent Search). Whereas the function of the business opportunity analysis section is to serve as a clearing house for ideas on promising business opportunities, the community relations section will serve as clearing house on individuals who might exploit these opportunities. This function will entail the careful screening of candidates and an assessment of their ability to handle business successfully.

Project Direction. This section brings the pieces together and performs the essential function of helping launch the business. With individuals screened through the community relations section and with business opportunities presented by the opportunity group, a project director is then in the position of designing a start-up. In addition, he will secure capital. (While it might be desirable to set up a separate capital section in the office, in most cases capital securement is a very specialized task and needs to be handled by the team helping organize the business.)

The project director will also arrange for various kinds of assistance for the new entrepreneur, either ongoing counseling or formal class training. These services would be arranged by the training and consulting coordinator.

Perhaps the best way to illustrate the role of the project director is to take a fairly concrete case—one that is in the offing at the present. The elements of this entrepreneurship are the following: several youth groups have expressed desires to operate businesses on their own; a group of lawyers would like to sponsor such businesses;

and a group of investors are willing to back the youth if the right opportunity can be found. With these ingredients and with the kind of direction that would be involved in the Small Business Development Office, it should be possible to put together a business opportunity that would have some chance of success. For example, it might be possible to work out a mimeographing contract with the University of Chicago. Alternatively, some type of community maintenance group, analogous to PRIDE[8] might be organized.

Management Assistance. This section will organize two types of services: one-to-one counseling and formal classroom activity. Both of these functions could probably be performed by other organizations such as students, alumni and faculty of the University of Chicago, Hyde Park residents, staff from local banks, and the like. A reasonably successful program of technical assistance has been in operation for several years at the Graduate School of Business at the University of Chicago. It is quite likely that a bilateral arrangement could be worked out between the SBDO and the student group at the university.

For classroom work, many possibilities exist in the Chicago area: courses run by the Board of Education and the junior colleges, occasional seminars by the University of Chicago, and evening programs by the Cosmopolitan Chamber of Commerce and Congressman Dawson (the latter two programs are supported by the SBA).

The concrete activities of a small business development office can be exemplified as follows:

(1) Investigate the possibility of establishing local insurance companies.

PROGRAMMATIC COMPONENTS

(2) Investigate the possibility of promoting a locally owned and operated recreational center, such as a swimming pool, a skating rink, etc.

(3) Investigate the feasibility of a credit-loan service for area residents.

(4) Provide equity funds for new or existing Negro businesses in Woodlawn. After the firm has performed successfully for a period of time and has gained community support, the development corporation could try to sell out its equity share to the community.

(5) Provide loans at low rates of interest for new or existing businesses in Woodlawn.

(6) Seek out Woodlawn residents who would be interested in entrepreneural opportunities.

(7) Develop a file of ideas for new businesses that would be feasible for Woodlawn.

(8) Help those white businessmen who wish to leave Woodlawn sell their businesses to Negroes.

(9) Promote the partnership idea to community residents and white businessmen in Woodlawn. There may be some white businessmen in the community who would welcome a Negro partner from the neighborhood. The development corporation could provide a loan for the black partners.

(10) Obtain (or develop) and publicize a list of Negro-owned businesses. Four lists might be desirable: production, wholesale, retail, and services.

(11) Encourage the city of Chicago, as well as churches, universities, businesses, etc., to place their accounts in banks that lend to Negro businessmen. The purchase of products or services of local firms could be handled in a similar way.

(12) Maintain a list of management advisors, accountants, and lawyers who would be willing to help Negro

businessmen solve their problems.

(13) Maintain a current file of all sources of funds that are available to Negro businessmen.

(14) Negotiate with the University of Chicago, the Chicago Junior College system, or other educational institutions, for the establishment of an intensive business training program for Negro businessmen. Project Outreach, under SBA funding, provides one such program which is free to small businessmen. Training should include management techniques, bookkeeping, marketing, government regulations, business data, advertising, location, decor, etc. The training program might also be established under the auspices of the CVI.

(15) Keep information on Negroes in other cities who are managing successful businesses. This information might be helpful to Woodlawn residents who would consider beginning a business.

(16) Promote marketing services for area businessmen.

(17) Develop franchise opportunities.

(18) Promote youth enterprises.

(19) Develop consumer cooperatives.

(20) Restrict the number of wholesale and retail liquor outlets established in the community.

Housing

Improved housing is central to the citizen's and community's perception of their status, and the principal means by which they judge personal and family achievement. However, use of housing improvement as the main instrument to achieve personal and family fulfillment is self-defeating. The supply of low-rental housing, sales of private housing, and the costs of rehabilitation and new construction make significant advances in this

PROGRAMMATIC COMPONENTS

area impossible in isolation. Massive public housing, which is one available alternative, is no longer acceptable to inner-city residents and, moreover, is not even perceived as adequate housing. Therefore, any substantial rehabilitation and new construction program must be synchronized with income-maintenance programs, job improvement programs, and other evidences of rising per capita and family incomes.

There are, however, a series of newly developed instruments and practices which provide the capacity to begin an affirmative program of housing improvement immediately, even though the pace cannot be accelerated beyond the income capacities of the current residents, who are the group this Model Cities plan is intended to serve.

Certain premises are clear: first, current Woodlawn residents, given their income and family age and size distribution, must be served; gross densities (generally at the level of the total population now residing in Woodlawn) must be maintained; and the community must not be turned into a high-rise canyon, even though adjustments in net density (on a block or lot basis) may be required.

A priori, the zoning, housing, building, fire, and health codes of the city of Chicago must be enforced—immediately and without qualification.

Second, individual absentee owners particularly, or preferably combinations of absentee owners controlling buildings concentrated in blocks or parts of blocks, should be forced to improve their properties, through use of new financial aids, including foundation sources, so that the resultant rents, or dwelling unit sales in the case of transformation to cooperatives and condominiums, are within the financial capacity of Woodlawn residents.

Third, every abandoned and derelict building in Woodlawn which cannot be rehabilitated and occupied should be cleared immediately, together with the clearance of nonresidential dilapidated buildings. Along with the vacant land now available, this should constitute a development package for new private rental and sales housing for Woodlawn residents. Hopefully, the new occupancy which will result, if done on a systematic basis, could vacate existing deteriorated buildings and permit either their rehabilitation, if salvageable, or their clearance for new construction for Woodlawn residents.

Fourth, every foundation should be approached to launch a systematic and wholesale building purchase and rehabilitation program.

Fifth, every institution in the area, the parochial churches and schools, the Drexel Home for the Aged, and all other private and semipublic institutions must be encouraged to use a part of their assets to go into purchase and rehabilitation partnerships with the community.

Sixth, an aggressive, large-scale action program must be launched to secure all of the rent supplement funds which can fairly be sought for Woodlawn, all of the new, "low-middle income home ownership funds," (the Senator Percy enactment), all of the available "turnkey funds," and such other available dollars recently made available through legislative actions and federal administrative rulings.

A physical plan using facilities and space as described above will shape the environment to serve the basic needs of the population. Specific operations include:

(1) Identifying uses for vacant areas, as well as the

new uses for land with buildings for which there is no alternative but clearance.

(2) Using the legal instruments discussed earlier to develop programs to deal with those buildings which are basically sound but which have been abused.

(3) Examining new uses for land in terms of the job-generating requirements of the population, the day-care requirements, and the needed educational facilities. Thus it is conceivable, for example, that the new school patterns will provide: schools placed in multiple-use structures in which housing, as well as other facilities, might be included; schools that might be tied in with job-creating facilities which might be constructed; and, at the other end of the age spectrum, the inclusion of the day-care centers discussed earlier as part of the normal educational system.

(4) Providing decent, desirable accommodations for typical Woodlawn residents, but especially for families with children. Realtors and property owners will not be permitted to discriminate against any Woodlawn residents, particularly large families.

(5) Encouraging home ownership by raising funds for mortgages and otherwise stimulating home ownership and the conversion of apartment dwellings to condominiums owned jointly by the tenants. The HED would also investigate the possibility of acquiring property for rental occupancy. Other sources of funding and mortgaging also would be sought.

Within this context of stimulating housing rehabilitation and new construction, the following steps are important:

(1) Obtain black contractors, wherever possible, to undertake new construction and rehabilitation in Woodlawn in accordance with the initial phases of the Model

Cities housing plan.

(2) Develop and manage a Comprehensive Building Maintenance Corporation (CBMC), which would ultimately be charged with the responsibility for rehabilitation in Woodlawn once such a corporation is operative. Apprenticeship programs should be set up and union membership obtained, where necessary, for workers. The CBMC will provide a source of employment for youth as well as a locus of job-training experience; its activities would thus be closely coordinated with the schools program and the CVI. The CBMC would respond to complaints about building violations, and would, therefore, maintain a close relationship with other agencies set up under Model Cities programs to respond to such complaints. The CBMC would rely on the Law Division within the Core as necessary.

(3) Provide special services to occupants to enable them to handle financial commitments of renovated units.

Program for Young People

The materials recited in this section are drawn from other parts of this document. They are collected here to outline a pattern of activity centering on the young adult which would have an independent identity, even though related to all other aspects of Model Cities planning. The unemployment among young people and their lack of educational achievement are commonly known and addressed statistically elsewhere in this document.

There are five components of a recommended Young Adult Program, which need to be viewed as an integral whole; each item is linked to all others:

Economic Development—small business (retail, wholesale, distributorships, service establishments, etc.) and small industrial establishments.

The opportunity exists via the proposed Housing and Economic Development Corporation to stimulate black entrepreneurship. The young adult could be involved as a member of a specially constituted board of this corporation to implement such activity.

In turn, this board would help secure capital and establish young adults in their own enterprises. The board would help them develop the expertise essential to business success by finding ways for them to acquire the managerial skill, knowledge, and confidence to assure long-term stability. The necessary training and the technical assistance would be provided by the Career Vocational Institute.

The Career Vocational Institute (CVI)—the young adults could be involved both on the policy councils of the Institute and as students in the Institute itself. The CVI will, as in connection with the fluid schools, view its programs as using the student as pupil, employee, and policy advisor. All of the activities of the CVI will be directed toward career goals for the young adult and be entwined with the black entrepreneurship activities, the employment placement activities, and the training activities.

Employment—related to entrepreneurship and the Career Vocational Institute, the Housing and Economic Development Corporation, in which the earlier recited activities would be organizationally situated, will establish an active employment placement service manned by young adults and others. Principal functions of this employment service will be to find placements for the young adults and to attract employment-generating establishments and industries in Woodlawn and adjacent areas which would create employment opportunities for these young people.

The Fluid Schools—for those young adults who seek an education and for whom the traditional and conventional school experience is inapplicable, a school program "outside the school" will be available. Schoolrooms in factories related to jobs with noneducator teachers, in hospitals and clinics, and in other more casual settings using nonconventional materials and teachers, as well as work-oriented teachers, are proposed.

It is recommended that the policy board for the fluid schools consist largely of young adults who would be paid for their time and be relied on to play a crucial part in the operation of the fluid schools. The experience of operating (in large measure) an independent school establishment may be valuable not only to young adults but also to professional educators.

Nonprofessional Staffs in the Core and the Pad—the opportunity exists to draw on the young adults as a major source of staffing to both the back-up facilities in the Core and as community workers in the Pad. Not only do the young adults have many of the talents required for these activities, but this approach could open up lifelong career opportunities for the young person within many of the traditional professional areas: health, law, social service, employment, education, etc.

There can be little doubt that new bureaucracies are in the making naturally—bureaucracies of nonprofessionals who in time will develop their own special skill patterns, qualifications, and requirements. What better resource of their creation than the young adult, currently alienated, angry, and outside the established system.

ACTION PROGRAM: FIRST YEAR

The costs of the programs proposed herein are high. Each of the recommended program elements may be difficult to achieve and will confront political, professional, and administrative resistance and constraints. But the Woodlawn community is playing the urban game and for the ultimate stakes—survival. The test is not dollar digestibility or ease of implementation, but the requirements of problem solving.

THE MAJOR AREAS OF FIRST-YEAR ACTIVITIES (SEVEN ELEMENTS)

(1) *During the crucial first year following approval of this Model Cities plan we propose that substantial amounts of time, energy, and resources be committed to marshalling the existing powers and tools of the city and applying them massively in the target area.* This will include a stepped-up code enforcement program, increased housekeeping activities (including trash collection and street cleaning), improved maintenance of the elevated train, streets and sidewalks, cleaning up of vacant lots, accelerated construction on the cleared urban-renewal sites, removal of all abandoned and derelict buildings and automobiles, attention to the most severe cases of building deterioration and overcrowding with particular emphasis on the rehousing of residents in standard housing in Woodlawn, increase in the alloca-

tion of rent supplement commitments, speed-up in the rehabilitation of Hyde Park High School, stimulation of private low-rise residential construction on currently vacant lots, and a freeze on high-rise residential construction. These and similar activities will be directed toward the stabilization of the community, the community morale-building which will reinforce citizen optimism with respect to the Model Cities prospect, and provide affirmative evidence of the city's good faith. It is also recommended that during the first year the Woodlawn Model Area Planning Council be reconstituted to include only residents of Woodlawn and representatives of legitimate Woodlawn organizations, and that a predominant number of the reconstituted council represent the community's major organization.

(2) *Pilot activities which will be directed toward two concurrent processes:*

(a) *Testing* of the variety of new ideas included in the strategy and program component sections in earlier parts of this document, i.e., scientific mode, the fluid schools, the income maintenance program, the "barometric"-oriented research, the neighborhood education and arbitration council, and other comparable pioneering proposals.

(b) *Operationalizing* all of the activities earlier recited, including the Core Corporation; the outreach facilities (the Pads); the schools proposed at a variety of age levels; the Career Vocational Institute; the evaluation survey; the Cultural and Language Arts Center; the Community Health Center; and, most important, the board, convenor and other elements of the Core superstructure. Operationalization will relate both to the initial undertaking of all the recited activities proposed in this document as well as for the total five-year term covered.

ACTION PROGRAM: FIRST YEAR

(3) *The launching of training activities* to begin providing the supply of needed nonprofessionals to man both the back-up functional facilities located in the Core as well as in the Pads.

(4) *The selection of the basic professional staff* for both the administrative as well as professional positions associated with all the activities referred to in connection with the Core and its functional divisions, the education system, and the Housing and Economic Development Corporation.

(5) Completing necessary steps in connection with *formation of the many public community corporations* proposed, particularly the Core Corporation as well as the Housing and Economic Development Corporation. In addition, putting together the necessary materials leading to the creating of the independently governed new hospital corporation.

(6) Detailed *planning for construction* will begin in the first stage for the construction of recommended facilities, particularly schools.

(7) *Space will be secured* to begin the coming operationalization with special attention to finding locations for the Core, the Pads, Community Health Centers, the Career Vocational Institute, and other facilities.

ACTION COMPONENTS IN THE FIRST-YEAR PROGRAM

Some of these items are spelled out in detail below; others are developed as part of the earlier included program component section in those instances in which a separation by phases would have destroyed the fabric of the program proposal.

(1) Study designs and other associated steps in connection with the actual launching and undertaking of the evaluation study will begin during this stage including design of questionnaires, pretesting, sampling, interviewing, coding, processing, and tabulation.

(2) Test examinations will be completed on the variety of new ideas earlier discussed and a judgment made as to whether to proceed in the face of such examinations, and in what form. This in relationship to such elements as the arbitration council, the fluid schools, scientific modeling, the Career Vocational Institute, the Cultural and Language Arts Center, etc.

(3) Legal services (as detailed in the law program component) will commence on all recited constituent elements of the legal component of the plan.

(4) A special demonstration will be established in connection with income maintenance using the Woodlawn Model Cities target area as a case-study area to determine the merit and feasibility of the plan as a critical step toward establishing its applicability to the total county welfare client group as well as the state and nation.

(5) As stated earlier, this phase will also include the creation, and the private and public funding, of the newly proposed public community corporations: the Core Corporation, and the Housing and Economic Development Corporation, particularly.

(6) The Core structure and the Pad structure will be fully activated as early during the first phase as feasible.

ACTION PROGRAM: FIRST YEAR

Footnotes

1. As noted in the prior section, the Social Service Clinic will constitute the social service backup facility in the Core. In time this function may be absorbed by the University of Chicago, School of Social Service Administration Social Service Center.

2. Morris Janowitz, "Institution Building in Urban Education," **Innovation in Mass Education,** ed. by David Street (To be published by John Wiley, 1968).

3. See Janowitz, **op. cit,;** Kenneth Clark, "Defeatism in Ghetto Schools," **School Children and the Urban Slum,** ed. by Joan I. Roberts (New York: The Free Press, 1967), pp. 599-611; and James S. Coleman, **et al., Equality of Educational Opportunity** (Washington, D.C.: U.S. Government Printing Office, 1966).

4. Morris Janowitz, **op. cit.**

5. **Experimental Schools in East Woodlawn: A Proposal** (Chicago: Urban Educatin Developmental Project, University of Chicago, November 30, 1967).

6. See the latest BLS report on the STATUS OF THE NEGRO.

7. Garth L. Mangum, "Reorienting Vocational Education," Wayne State University: The Institute of Labor and Industrial Relations, Policy Papers in Human Resources and Industrial Relations, No. 7.

8. This Washington D.C. group has received several hundred thousand dollars in funds from the U.S. Department of Labor.

APPENDIX

MEMBERS OF THE WOODLAWN ORGANIZATION AND RESIDENTS OF THE GREATER WOODLAWN COMMUNITY (CENTRAL WOODLAWN, EAST CENTRAL WOODLAWN, EAST WOODLAWN, WEST WOODLAWN, NORTH WOODLAWN, WASHINGTON PARK, PARKSIDE, ESSEX AND SOUTH SHORE) WHO COMPRISED THE T.W.O. MODEL CITIES PLANNING COUNCIL

Rev. Arthur M. Brazier, Apostolic Church of God

Mr. Bolin V. Bland, Evans-Langley Neighborhood Club

Mrs. Phillis Hubbard, D.M.C. Neighborhood Improvement Club

Mrs. Kate Talley, D.M.C. Neighborhood Improvement Club

Mr. William Smith, 6300 Maryland Block Club

Mrs. Catherine Smith, 6300 Maryland Block Club

Mrs. Saphronia Terrell, I.D.E. Club

Mr. Leon Cammon, I.D.D. Club

Mrs. Rosa Scott, 6300 Drexel Block Club

Mrs. Mary Booth, 6300 Drexel Block Club

APPENDIX

Mrs. Ida Davis, 6500 University Block Club

Mr. James Grammer, 6500 University Block Club

Mr. Lee Smith, 6500 Greenwood Block Club

Mrs. Dolores Easter, 6500 Greenwood Block Club

Mr. Aubrey Stanley, 6500 Woodlawn-Minerva Block Club

Rev. Oliver Harvey, 6500 Woodlawn-Minerva Block Club

Mr. Orville Fitzgerald, Woodlawn Block Club Council, Inc.

Mr. Wiley Moore, 6500 Ellis Block Club

Mrs. Marguaritte Frazier, 6500 Ellis Block Club

Mrs. Helen Warfield, 6400 Woodlawn Block Clu

Sister M. Alissa, 6400 Woodlawn Block Club

Mr. Albert Craig, The Blacks

Mrs. Cynthia Dawkins, The·Blacks

Rev. John Baggett, Woodlawn Methodist Church

Mr. Leon Miles, Woodlawn Methodist Church

Rev. Graves, Christ Deliverance Church

Mr. Walter Jones, 7400 Kimbark Block Club

Rev. Hiram Crawford, Israel Methodist Church

Mr. Eugene Morris, Israel Methodist Church

Rev. Richard Deines, Woodlawn Lutheran Church

Mrs. Evelyn Shropshire, Woodlawn Lutheran Church

Rev. John Dribelbus, Christ Episcopal Church

Mr. James Terry, Christ Episcopal Church

Rev. John Fry, First Presbyterian Church

Rev. Harold Walker, First Presbyterian Church

Rev. Carlos Jarvis, Parkside Baptist Church

Mr. Joseph Warsham, Parkside Baptist Church

Rev. Tracy O'Sullivan, St. Cyril's Roman Catholic Church

Mrs. Risa Gardner, St. Cyril's Roman Catholic Church

Rev. Bellermine Wilson, St. Clara's Roman Catholic Church

Mrs. Rose Stanley, St. Clara's Roman Catholic Church

Rev. Lester Bell, Christ Deliverence Church

Mr. George Banks, Christ Deliverence Church

Rev. Bernard Guirsch, St. Laurence Roman Catholic Church

Mrs. Jessie Jones, St. Laurence Roman Catholic Church

Rev. William T. Baird, Essex Community Church

Mrs. Mildred Shelby, Essex Community Church

Mrs. Annie Jackson, T.W.O. Social Welfare Union

Mrs. Elvira Grover, T.W.O. Social Welfare Union

Mrs. Carrie Green, T.W.O. Social Welfare Union

APPENDIX

Mrs. Betty Jackson, T.W.O. Social Welfare Union

Mrs. Lena Goodman, T.W.O. Social Welfare Union

Mrs. Violet Robinson, T.W.O. Social Welfare Union

Mrs. Dorothy Chivers, T.W.O. Social Welfare Union

Mrs. Addie Garel, T.W.O. Social Welfare Union

Mrs. Mavis Dancey, T.W.O. Social Welfare Union

Mrs. Freddie Butler, T.W.O. Social Welfare Union

Mrs. Betty Van Hook, T.W.O. Social Welfare Union

Mrs. Mattie Preston, Lively Workers

Mr. Andrew Taylor, Lively Workers

Mr. Harlan Hayes, 6300-6400 Ellis Block Club

Rev. Lee Koonce, Parkway Christian Church

Mrs. Mamie Martin, Evans-Langley Neighborhood Club

Mrs. Glen Jones, 6100-6200 King Drive Block Club

Mrs. B. Gordon Moore, 6100-6200 King Drive Block Club

Mrs. Carrie Little, 6100-6200 Rhodes Block Club

Attorney Lawrence Carroll, Westenders

Mr. Mack McEwen, West Woodlawn Improvement Organization

Mr. Fred Engram, West Woodlawn Improvement Organization

Rev. Thomas Ellis, Lincoln Memorial Congregational Church

Mr. Hill, 6700 Champlain Block Club

Mr. L. Carrington, 6700 Champlain Block Club

Mr. A. L. Smith, Woodlawn Citizens Improvement Organization, Inc.

Mr. O. B. Williams, Woodlawn Citizens Improvement Organization, Inc.

Mrs. Rosa Mims, Essex-Blackstone Improvement Association

Mrs. Marie Lynch, Essex-Blackstone Improvement Association

Mr. Nathaniel Love, 7500 Dorchester Block Club

Mrs. Eula Mae Anderson, 7500 Dorchester Block Club

Mrs. Constance Bogan, 7400 Kenwood Block Club

Mr. Johnnie Crittle, 7400 Kenwood Block Club

Mr. Joseph McCurry, Grand Crossing Improvement Association

Mrs. Eloise Hart, Observer Civic Club

Mrs. Elizabeth Sawyer, Observer Civic Club

Mrs. Catherine Croff, South Shore Progressives

Mrs. Carrie Ray, Dor-Stone Block Club

Mrs. Gertrude Coward, Dor-Stone Block Club

Mrs. Hester Smith, Preschool Parent Council

Mrs. Ammie Patton, Preschool Parent Council

APPENDIX

Mrs. Edith Wilder, Preschool Parent Council

Mrs. Alice Walker, Preschool Parent Council

Mrs. Mary Jackson, Preschool Parent Council

Mrs. Mary L. King, Preschool Parent Council

Mrs. Dolores Kelly, Preschool Parent Council

Mrs. Betty Jean Johnson, Preschool Parent Council

Mrs. Johnnie Turner, Preschool Parent Council

Mrs. Zephyr Craddock, Parkway Gardens

Mrs. Mae Marton, Parkway Gardens

Mr. Earl Byrd, Parkway Gardens

Mr. Darnell James, Parkway Gardens

Mrs. Worday Blair, Parkway Gardens

Mrs. Norma Day, Parkway Gardens

Mr. Samuel Dixon, Parkway Gardens

Mrs. Thomas Wilkins, Parkway Gardens

Mr. Marshall Stern, Woodlawn Businessmen's Association

Mr. Harold Anderson, Woodlawn Businessmen's Association

Mr. Morris Kaplan, Woodlawn Businessmen's Association

Mr. George Kyros, Woodlawn Businessmen's Association

Mrs. Owyous Taylor, Marquette Civic Leaders

Mrs. Edna Jackson, Marquette Civic Leaders

Mrs. Viola Cotton, Concerned Parents of Scott School

Mrs. Willie B. Sims, Concerned Parents of Scott School

Mr. Charles Collins, Jackson Park Businessmen's Association

Mr. Romaine Blobaum, Jackson Park Businessmen's Association

Mr. Connie Monard, Jackson Park Businessmen's Association

APPENDIX

UNIVERSITY OF CHICAGO FACULTY AND STUDENTS WHO MADE TECHNICAL AND CONSULATIVE CONTRIBUTIONS TO DEVELOPING THE PLAN

ECONOMIC DEVELOPMENT

Robert B. McKersie, Professor, Graduate School of Business

Arnold R. Weber, Professor and Director of Research, Graduate School of Business

Robert L. Farwell, Associate Dean for Planning, Graduate School of Business, and Professorial Lecturer on Government and Business

EDUCATION

Roald Campbell, William Claude Reavis, Professor and Chairman, Department of Education; Dean, Graduate School of Education

Willard J. Congreve, Associate Professor, Department of Education, and Director, Woodlawn Experimental Schools District Project

Bruce MacPherson, Staff Associate, Graduate School of Education

William Boyd, Student, Graduate School of Education

WOODLAWN'S MODEL CITIES PLAN

HEALTH

Dr. Robert S. Daniels, Associate Dean of Social and Community Medicine in the Division of the Biological Sciences and the Pritzker School of Medicine, Associate Professor, Department of Psychiatry

Prof. Charles R. Goulet, Director of the University Hospitals and Clinics; Professor and Associate Director, Hospital Administration Program, Graduate School of Business

Dr. John D. Madden, Assistant Professor, Department of Pediatrics, and Medical Director, Woodlawn Child Health Clinic

Dr. Sheppard G. Kellam, Associate Professor, Department of Psychiatry, and Co-Director, Woodlawn Mental Health Center

Dr. Sheldon Schiff, Associate Professor, Department of Psychiatry, and Co-Director, Woodlawn Mental Health Center

Dr. Joseph R. Swartwout, Associate Professor, Department of Obstetrics and Gynecology

Dr. Alvin R. Tarlov, Associate Professor and Acting Chairman, Department of Medicine

William Docken, Medical Student, Pritzker School of Medicine

LAW

Phillip Ginsberg, Director, Edwin F. Mandel Legal Aid Clinic, and Assistant Professor, Law School

Patrick A. Keenan, Graduate Student, Law School

William Parks, Graduate Student, Law School

Philip A. Verveer, Graduate Student, Law School

James P. Walsh, Graduate Student, Law School

James Gray, Consultant, Practicing Attorney

Fred C. Blackledge, Consultant, Practicing Attorney

SOCIAL SERVICES

Harold A. Richman, Assistant Professor, School of Social Services Administration

Larry Johnson, Graduate Student, School of Social Services Administration

Lynn Vogel, Graduate Student, School of Social Services Administration

Robert Whitby, Consultant, Booz, Allen & Hamilton, Inc.

OVERALL COORDINATION

Brian J. L. Berry, Professor, Department of Geography, and Chairman, Training Programs, Center for Urban Studies

Morris Janowitz, Professor and Chairman, Department of Sociology; Director of the Center for Social Organization Studies

Julian H. Levi, Professor of Urban Studies, Division of the Social Sciences; Executive Director, South East Chicago Commission

Jack Meltzer, Professor of Urban Studies, Division of the Social Sciences, and Director, Center for Urban Studies

Richard Appelbaum, Graduate Student, Department of Sociology

Thomas Philpott, Graduate Student, Department of History

William Swenson, Graduate Student, Committee on the Analysis of Ideas and the Study of Methods; Fellow of the Center for Urban Studies

CENTRAL STUDENT TASK FORCE

Richard Appelbaum, Graduate Student, Department of Sociology

Gene O. Armstrong, Graduate Student, Graduate School of Business

Alan Jaffe, Graduate Student, Graduate School of Business

Jeffrey Kuta, College, Sociology

John Perry, College, Public Affairs

Thomas Philpott, Graduate Student, Department of History; Fellow, Center for Urban Studies

John Ryan, College, Public Affairs

William Swenson, Graduate Student, Committee on the Analysis of Ideas and the Study of Methods; Fellow, Center for Urban Studies

Thomas Unterman, Graduate Student, University of Chicago Law School

Barbara Yondorf, College, Public Affairs

APPENDIX

MEMBERS OF THE T.W.O. TASK FORCE COMMITTEES FOR MODEL CITIES PLANNING

WAYS AND MEANS COMMITTEE - For coordination of all committee work

Rev. Arthur M. Brazier, T.W.O. President, Committee Chairman

All Task Force Committee Chairmen and Vice-Chairmen

Mr. Leon D. Finney, T.W.O. Staff Director, Community Technical Advisor

TASK FORCE COMMITTEES

HOUSING COMMITTEE - Environmental Planning

Mr. Andrew Smith, Chairman

Mr. Andrew Taylor, Co-Chairman

Mr. Lee Langster, Vice-Chairman

Mr. Andrew Preer, Community Technical Advisor

SCHOOLS COMMITTEE - Education and Recreation

Mr. Noel Alsbrook, Chairman

Mrs. Viola Cotton, Vice-Chairman

Mrs. Rosie Simpson, Community Technical Advisor

APPENDIX

Mrs. L. K. McClelland, Community Technical Advisor

CIVIL RIGHTS COMMITTEE - Legal Aid

Attorney E. Duke McNeil, Chairman

Mr. Joseph Warsham, Vice-Chairman

Mr. James Wethers, Community Technical Advisor

FUND RAISING COMMITTEE AND CONSUMER PRACTICES COMMITTEE - Economic Development and Job Training

Mrs. Phillis Hubbard, Chairman, Consumer Practices

Mrs. Worday Blair, Chairman, Fund Raising

Mrs. Mamie Martin, Vice-Chairman

Mr. Leon D. Finney, T.W.O. Staff Director, Community Technical Advisor

Mr. Donald M. Androzzo, O.J.T. Project Director, Community Technical Advisor

SOCIAL WELFARE COMMITTEE - Financial and Social Services

Jannie Nash, Co-Chairman

Annie Jackson, Co-Chairman

Addie Garel, Vice-Chairman

Mrs. Joyce Carter, Community Technical Assistant

HEALTH COMMITTEE - Health Services and Outreach Systems

Mrs. Brenda Coleman, Chairman

Mrs. Dorothy Chivers, Vice-Chairman

Mr. Joseph W. Jenkins, Community Technical Assistant

TABLE 3

SUMMARY

FIRST THROUGH FIFTH YEAR

	Financial Assistance and Social Service	Evaluation and Research	Housing and Economic Development	Education, Culture, and Recreation	Health	Legal	Overall Administration*	Funds Totals
TOTAL COST:	$17,171,000	$2,393,000	$36,370,560	$56,878,537	$27,207,600	$3,382,500	$2,619,500	$146,022,697
Total Funds Available:								
Non-Federal	3,603,000		9,372,000	26,893,550	6,525,000	522,000		46,915,550
Federal Non-Supplementary	11,631,525		12,989,700	9,249,600	12,200,500	1,299,000		47,370,325
Supplementary Model Cities	1,936,475	2,393,000	14,008,860	20,735,387	8,482,100	1,561,500	2,619,500	51,736,822
TOTAL FUNDS:	17,171,000	2,393,000	36,370,560	56,878,537	27,207,600	3,382,500	2,619,500	146,022,697

*These funds constitute programmatic monies in their own right. They should not be viewed as administrative expenses as that term is usually used.

TABLE 4

OVERALL

FIRST YEAR SUMMARY

	Financial Assistance and Social Service	Evaluation and Research	Housing and Economic Development	Education, Culture, and Recreation	Health	Legal	Overall Administration*	Functional Totals
TOTAL COST:	$3,577,000	$483,000	$8,639,128	$5,119,200	$446,200	$569,300	$532,700	$19,366,528
Total Funds Available:								
Non-Federal	1,288,000		2,600,000	1,357,500	125,000	68,400		5,438,900
Federal Non-Supplementary	1,814,305		4,200,300	1,216,600	200,500	229,000		7,660,705
Supplementary Model Cities	474,695	483,000	1,838,828	2,545,100	120,700	271,900	532,700	6,266,923
TOTAL FUNDS:	3,577,000	483,000	8,639,128	5,119,200	446,200	569,300	532,700	19,366,528

*These funds constitute programmatic monies in their own right. They should not be viewed as administrative expenses as that term is usually defined.

TABLE 5

TOTAL FUNDING SUMMARY - SECOND THROUGH FIFTH YEARS

	Financial Assistance and Social Service	Evaluation and Research	Housing and Economic Development	Education, Culture, and Recreation	Health	Legal	Overall Administration*	Program Totals
TOTAL COST:	$13,594,000	$1,910,000	$27,731,432	$51,759,337	$26,761,400	$2,813,200	$2,086,800	$126,656,169
Total Funds Available:								
Non-Federal	2,315,000		6,772,000	25,536,050	6,400,000	453,600		41,476,650
Federal Non-Supplementary	9,817,220		8,789,400	8,033,000	12,000,000	1,070,000		39,709,620
Supplementary Model Cities	1,461,780	1,910,000	12,170,032	18,190,287	8,361,400	1,289,600	2,086,800	45,469,899
TOTAL FUNDS:	13,594,000	1,910,000	27,731,432	51,759,337	26,761,400	2,813,200	2,086,800	126,656,169

*These funds constitute programmatic monies in their own right. They should not be viewed as administrative expenses as that term is usually used.

MAP 1.

THE COMMUNITY OF WOODLAWN WITHIN THE CITY OF CHICAGO

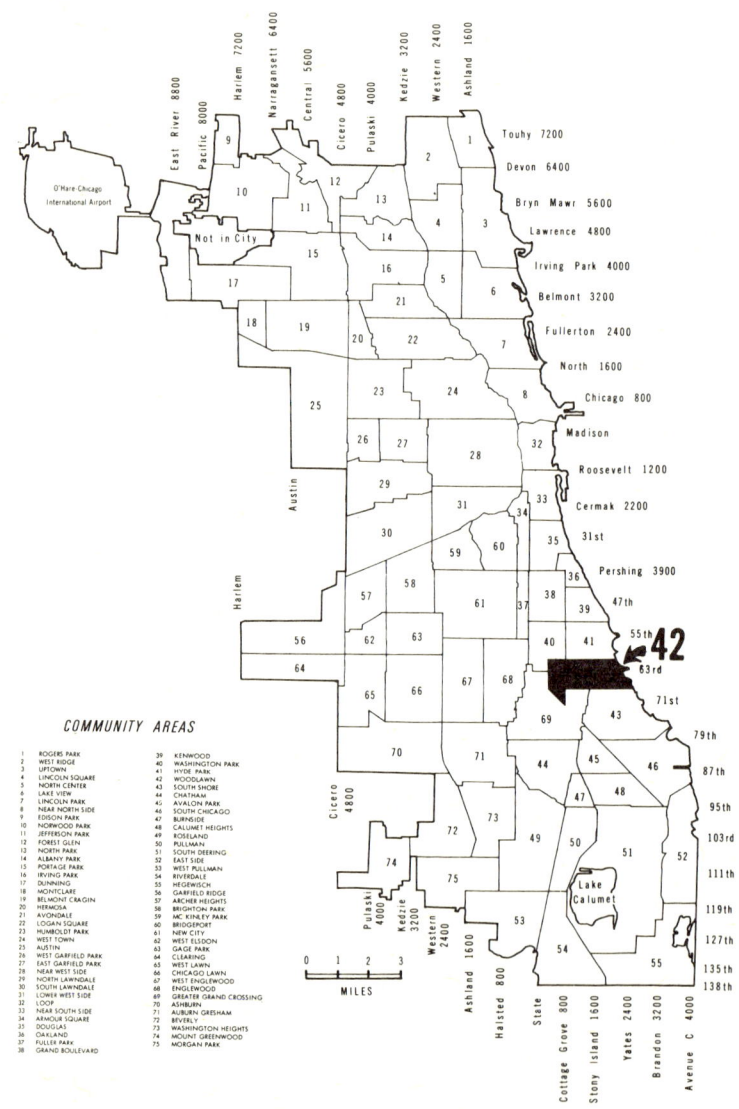

Prepared by the Center for Urban Studies, University of Chicago. Boundaries are for 1968

MAP 2.
THE GREATER WOODLAWN AREA

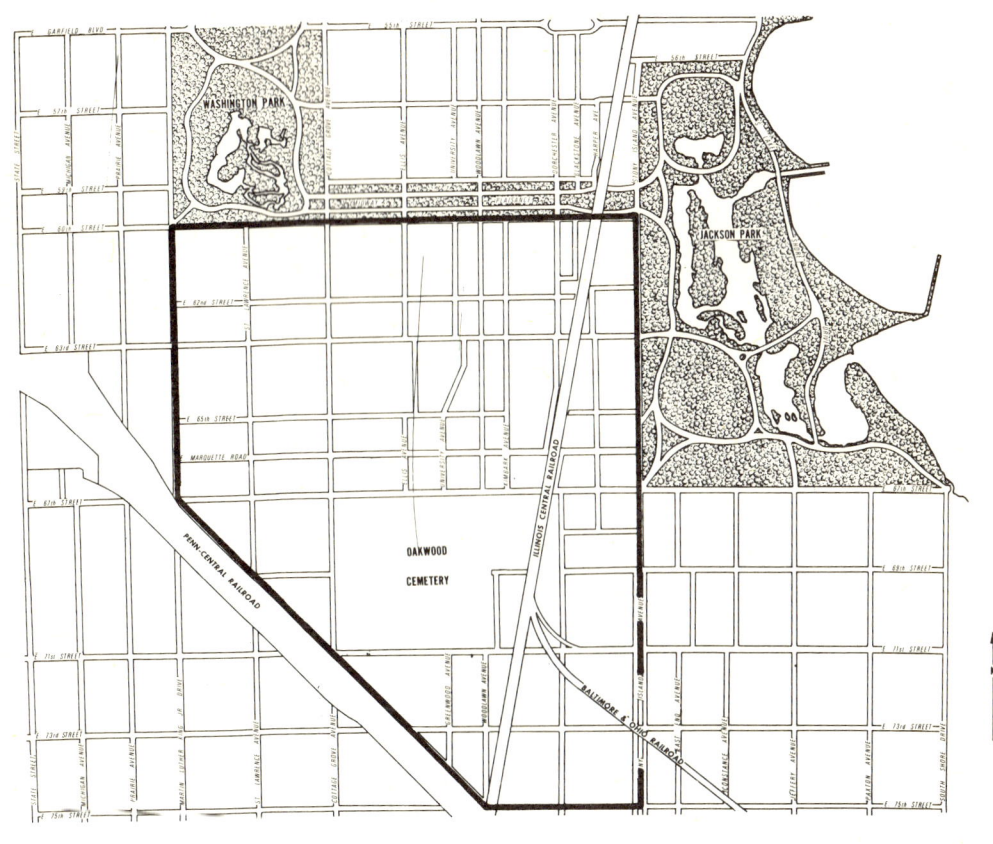

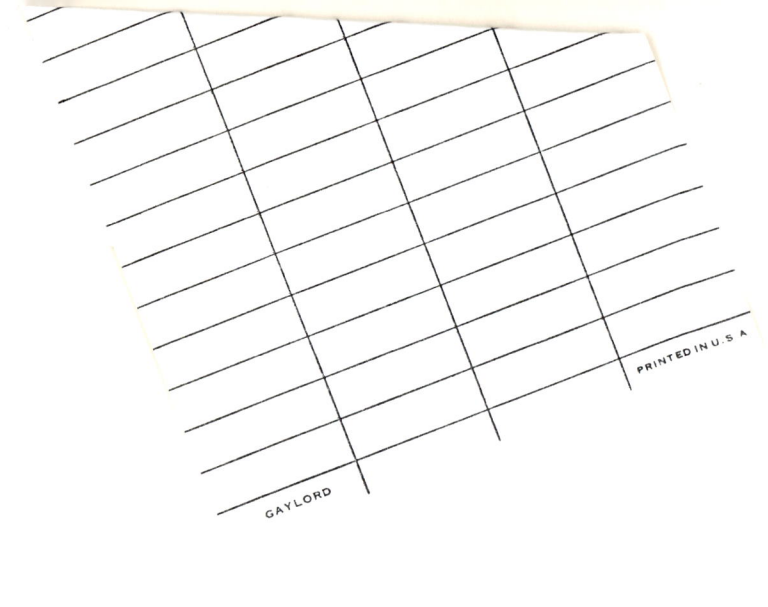